THIRTY YEARS FROM HOME:
A Seaman's View of the
War of 1812

THIRTY YEARS FROM HOME:
A Seaman's View of the
War of 1812

by

Samuel Leech

Fireship Press
www.FireshipPress.com

Thirty Years from Home: A Seaman's View of the War of 1812 - Copyright © 2008 by Fireship Press

ISBN-13: 978-1-934757-38-3
ISBN-10: 1-934757-38-1

BISAC Subject Headings:
  BIO008000 BIOGRAPHY & AUTOBIOGRAPHY / Military
  BIO006000 BIOGRAPHY & AUTOBIOGRAPHY / Historical
  BIO026000 BIOGRAPHY & AUTOBIOGRAPHY / Personal Memoirs

This work is based on the 1909 reprint of the 1843 edition of *Thirty Years from Home or A Voice from the Main Deck* by Samuel Leech, Boston: Tappan & Dennet.

Address all correspondence to:
Fireship Press
P.O. Box 68412
Tucson, AZ 85737
info@FireshipPress.com

Or visit our website at:
www.FireshipPress.com

1.0

PREFACE

I have often been solicited, by my personal friends, to commit the incidents of my life to paper. It was thought that they contained sufficient interest to command public attention. At any rate, there is a novelty in the fact of an unlettered sailor's appearance before the public, detailing the secrets of the naval Main Deck. The Quarter Deck has long and often told its own story, and has given its own coloring to naval life. Here, however, is a voice from the main deck, revealing life in a man of war as it appears to the sailor himself. As such, this work has some claim on the attention of the public.

I have endeavored to state facts as they were when I was a sailor, and in the ships to which I belonged. My object is to give a true picture. That, I have done, as far as a remarkably strong memory enabled me. I kept no journals, and consequently some slight mistakes in names, dates and places, may be found in my book; but I have been careful to state nothing as *facts,* of which I was not certain.

That the naval service has improved since I belonged to it, is, I believe, universally admitted. I rejoice at it. Still, it is not yet what it should be. If this work should, in any degree, stir up the public mind to amend the condition of seamen, I shall feel gratified, and fully repaid for the labor of placing these facts on record.

With many prayers that the perusal of these pages may do good, I leave the reader to pursue his way along the track of my experience: assuring him, that what may afford him pleasure to read, has cost me much pain to suffer.

Samuel Leech.

RECOMMENDATIONS

From the Hon. Erastus Corning.

Albany, N.Y., December 3, 1842.

To whom it may concern:

I have known and have had intercourse with Mr. Samuel Leech, for the last twenty years, and have always found him honorable in his dealings, and consider him entitled to the confidence of the public as a man of strict integrity.

ERASTUS CORNING.

The undersigned, being acquainted with Mr. Samuel Leech, the author of the following work, do cheerfully vouch for his moral and Christian character; and assure the public, that the interesting volume, which he here presents to the world, may be relied upon as an honest statement of facts, with which the writer was personally conversant; and as having no fellowship whatever with those fictitious tales of the sea, which, under the garb and professions of truth, have been proffered to the reading community.

CHARLES ADAMS,
Principal Wes. Academy.

JOHN BOWERS,
Pastor Cong. Church,
Wilbraham, Mass.

Wilbraham, May 4, 1843.

DAVID PATTEN,
Pastor, Providence, R. I.

REUBEN RANSOM,
Presiding Elder,
Springfield Dis. N. E. C.

HENRY CHASE,
Preacher to Seamen, N. Y.

RECOMMENDATIONS

From the Hon. Erastus Corning.

Albany, N.Y., December 3, 1842.

To whom it may concern:
I have known and have had intercourse with Mr. Samuel Leech, for the last twenty years, and have always found him honorable in his dealings, and consider him entitled to the confidence of the public as a man of strict integrity.

ERASTUS CORNING.

The undersigned, being acquainted with Mr. Samuel Leech, the author of the following work, do cheerfully vouch for his moral and Christian character; and assure the public, that the interesting volume, which he here presents to the world, may be relied upon as an honest statement of facts, with which the writer was personally conversant; and as having no fellowship whatever with those fictitious tales of the sea, which, under the garb and professions of truth, have been proffered to the reading community.

CHARLES ADAMS,
Principal Wes. Academy.

JOHN BOWERS,
Pastor Cong. Church,
Wilbraham, Mass.

Wilbraham, May 4, 1843.

DAVID PATTEN,
Pastor, Providence, R. I.

REUBEN RANSOM,
Presiding Elder,
Springfield Dis. N. E. C.

HENRY CHASE,
Preacher to Seamen, N. Y.

PREFACE

I have often been solicited, by my personal friends, to commit the incidents of my life to paper. It was thought that they contained sufficient interest to command public attention. At any rate, there is a novelty in the fact of an unlettered sailor's appearance before the public, detailing the secrets of the naval Main Deck. The Quarter Deck has long and often told its own story, and has given its own coloring to naval life. Here, however, is a voice from the main deck, revealing life in a man of war as it appears to the sailor himself. As such, this work has some claim on the attention of the public.

I have endeavored to state facts as they were when I was a sailor, and in the ships to which I belonged. My object is to give a true picture. That, I have done, as far as a remarkably strong memory enabled me. I kept no journals, and consequently some slight mistakes in names, dates and places, may be found in my book; but I have been careful to state nothing as *facts,* of which I was not certain.

That the naval service has improved since I belonged to it, is, I believe, universally admitted. I rejoice at it. Still, it is not yet what it should be. If this work should, in any degree, stir up the public mind to amend the condition of seamen, I shall feel gratified, and fully repaid for the labor of placing these facts on record.

With many prayers that the perusal of these pages may do good, I leave the reader to pursue his way along the track of my experience: assuring him, that what may afford him pleasure to read, has cost me much pain to suffer.

Samuel Leech.

ORIGINAL EDITOR'S PREFACE

NARRATIVES of service, a century ago, written by private soldiers, are rare, but such by common sailors are almost unknown. Samuel Leech's narrative *Thirty Years from Home, a voice from the Main-Deck* is a unique book, and now scarce. It is a valuable contribution to our history, giving a sailor's experience in both British and American navies, and being the sole account by a British seaman of the capture of the *Macedonian* by the *United States,* in 1812.

The revelations he makes of the cruel treatment of their men by British naval officers are unfortunately matched by the similar account of life on the same frigate *United States,* then under command of *"Captain Claret"* in 1843-44, given by Herman Melville in his remarkable book *White Jacket, or the World in a Man of War.* Though he is writing of an era thirty years later than Leech's, the picture is equally distressing.

Leech also gives almost as bad a character to Captain David Porter (father of the late Admiral David D. Porter) as to the British tyrants.

It should be recorded in this connection, that flogging was abolished in the United States navy in 1851, through the efforts of Commodore Robert P. Stockton.

The book has never been reprinted before since its original appearance (1843.)

Editor.

—The late Rear Admiral S. R. Franklin *(Memories of a Rear Admiral,* 1898), who was midshipman on the *United States* when Herman Melville was of the crew, says *Captain Claret* was Captain James Armstrong, and the *Commodore* Thomas Ap Catesby Jones. He adds: "Melville's *White Jacket* had more influence in abolishing corporal punishment in the Navy than anything else. A copy of it was placed on the desk of every member of Congress, and was a most eloquent appeal to the humane sentiment of the country."

CHAPTER ONE

WERE it not that the most common of all inquiries, respecting every man who comes before the public, is, "who is he? whence did he proceed? who were his parents?" etc, I would not detain the reader with any account of my humble ancestors and their circumstances. But, since men naturally expect this information, and would hence consider my narrative imperfect without it, I shall take the liberty to introduce them.

My father's occupation was that of *valet de chambre* to Lord William Fitzroy, son of the Duke of Grafton. My recollections concerning him are few and indistinct, as he died while I was yet scarcely three years old. One little incident alone reminds me of wearing a mourning dress as a memento of sorrow for his death. Returning from the parish church in Walthamstow, I observed the larger boys amusing themselves by swinging across the rails of the fences; endeavoring to join in their amusement, my hands slipped, and falling into a muddy ditch, I nearly finished my course, ere it was well begun, by a violent death. A benevolent stranger, however, rescued me, and once safe, my grief for the sad condition of my little black frock was excessive and inconsolable. A trifling cause for sorrow, to be sure, yet men and women often grieve for causes equally contemptible.

Although my personal remembrances of my father's death are so indistinct, yet the frequent mention made of him by my mother, has left the pleasing impression on my mind that he died a Christian. "I have thought of my numerous sins, but God has forgiven them all. Be not troubled, for the Lord will provide for you and your children. You need not fear to leave me, for I am not alone; God is with me, though you are out of the room," were among his dying expressions; when, after fourteen months' endurance of the pains which accompany a slow consumption, he approached "that bourne from which no traveller returns." I expect to find my honored father in heaven.

Wanstead, in Essex, about seven miles from the great metropolis of England, was the town, and 1798 the year, of my birth. Were it necessary to designate the place more particularly, it might be said that the part of Wanstead where I first struggled into being, was called Nightingale Place; a most musical name, conferred in honor of the nightingales which abounded in the vicinity.

Two years subsequently to my father's demise, my mother became an inmate of the family of Lady Francis Spencer, daughter of the Duke of Grafton, and wife of Lord Spencer. As a consequence of this event, I was deprived of a mother's care and consigned to the charge of my aunt Turner, whose family amounted to the very respectable number of twenty-two sons and two daughters. The transfer of a child from the care of its parent to that of another person, may appear, at first sight, to be a very unimportant Incident; but trifling as it seems, it often exerts an influence which very materially changes the destiny of the child: it was so in my case. Most of my cousins were sailors, and some of them were constantly returning home, bringing, with true sailors' munificence, the pleasing and curious productions of distant climes as presents to their parents and friends; then, seated round the bright hearth-side, they used to tell of wild adventures and hairbreadth escapes, spinning out the winter evening's tale to the infinite delight of their willing listeners. Poor fellows! three of them died at sea; two more, John and Richard, perished in the ill-fated *Blenheim,* a seventy-four gun ship of the British navy, which went down off the Cape of Good Hope, with seven hundred as brave men on board as ever trod a plank. Notwithstanding these sad recollections, and though none perceived it, my three years' residence among these "sailors bold" decided the nature of my future calling; it captivated my imagination and begat a curiosity, which ultimately led me to make my "home upon the bounding deep."

An orphan is ever exposed to changes. The loss of either parent calls for a degree of sympathy and kindness from others, which they are rarely willing to expend except on their own. Such is the almost universal selfishness of human nature. My experience affords a verification of the truthfulness of the remark. For some cause or other, it became inconvenient for me to remain with my kind aunt Turner, and my next home was with a widowed aunt, at Wanstead, where I did not meet with the same kindness of treatment. The breaking of a cup, or any of the thousand-and-one offenses found in the list of juvenile defects, was sure to bring upon me the infliction of the rod; and, what was equally painful, my most economical aunt exacted the full payment for all these losses from the little pocket money I obtained by holding a horse, running errands, or as new-year and Christmas presents; thus gratifying her temper and her covetousness at once, besides embittering, to some extent, the boyish hours of my unfortunate self.

There is no evil in the management of children to be more deprecated than that species of treatment which tends to destroy their happiness. Correction for obvious faults, in a proper manner, is essential to their proper moral training; but a habit of incessantly scolding them for every little accident or offense, only serves to excite the growth of evil passions and to make them dislike their home; things to be avoided as much as Scylla and Charybdis by the careful mariner. The influence of such maltreatment follows the child through life, like an evil genius, materially affecting his views of life and the temper of his mind. For aught that now occurs to me, but for this unkindness, my early predilection for the sea would have died within me; while, as it was, I panted to enjoy the freedom my fancy painted in its pictures of sailor life. To add to my sorrows, my mother removed my sister, who had been my cheerful companion and true friend, to a lady's school at Woodstock, in Oxfordshire, for the twofold purpose of affording her greater literary advantages, and of being able to see her more frequently.

Several incidents occurred during my abode here, which tended to increase my growing desire. A smart, active sailor, over six feet in height, and well-proportioned, one day presented himself at my aunt's door. He told us he had been to America, where he had seen a young man named George Turner, who was her nephew and my cousin. He proceeded to tell many fine stories about him, and at last inquired if she should not like to see him, and if she should know him.

"I don't know as I should," said my aunt, "he has been away so long."

"Well, then," replied he, "I am George Turner! "

This fine, bold seaman, then, was my own cousin, son to my

aunt Turner; he had been eleven years at sea, and, after visiting his parents, took this method of surprising his aunt. Most likely he has made this adventure the subject of many a forecastle yarn since then. While he remained he was so jolly, so liberal, and so full of pleasant stories, that I began to feel quite sure that sailors were noble fellows.

We were also favored with a visit from an uncle, then visiting Europe from the West Indies. He was one of two brothers, who were educated at Greenwich for the navy. One of them had entered the British navy, and by dint of merit and hard service rose to the possession of a commission in the service, but ultimately perished at sea. This one had chosen the merchant service, but afterwards settled at Antigua. He took me with him to London, and carried me over the West India docks; he being well acquainted with many of the captains, they treated me with playful attention, inquiring if I did not wish to be a cabin-boy, and the like When I returned to Wanstead, it was with a stronger desire than ever to be a sailor. My uncle went to Trinidad, and died shortly after.

A very pleasant piece of intelligence greeted me soon after these incidents; it was nothing less than my removal from the care of my unkind aunt to the roof of my mother. Weary of her widowhood, she had again become a wife. My new parent was a widower with one son; a carpenter by occupation, in the employ of the Duke of Marlborough. Great was my joy when this fact was communicated to my young mind. I hailed it as a deliverance from bondage, and with beaming eyes and cheerful face hurried to bid adieu to my classmates in the day and in the Sunday school—a sad proof of the unfitness of my aunt for her task; since a child properly treated, will love its *home* too well to quit it without a tear; and if parents and guardians wish to prevent their children from being wanderers and stragglers through the wide world, let me bid them exert the utmost effort to make their home pleasant. Throw a charm round it, make it enchanted ground, cause it to become, in the language of a living poet,

The fairy ring of bliss

and then your children will love it too well to wander.

But I was now about to leave Wanstead, and, although delighted to be rid of the surveillance of a cross old relation, there were some things which threw an air of sadness occasionally over my mind. There were many pleasant associations connected with the place; its beautiful park, with herds of timid deer grazing under its tall oaks, upon whose green old heads the sun had shone for centuries; the venerable mansion, seated like a queen amid the sylvan scene; the old parish church, with its gorgeously painted windows, to which I had often walked on the Sabbath with my fellow-scholars in the Sabbath school, and beside whose deep-toned organ I had sat listening to the learned priest; the annual hunt at Easter, in which I had often joined the crew of idle lads that gave chase to the distracted deer; and the pleasant walks, made cheerful by the songs of innumerable birds, in Epping forest, were all to be left—perhaps forever. This thought made me somewhat sad, but it was swallowed up in the joy I felt when my mother appeared to conduct me to Bladen, some sixty miles from London, which was the place of her abode since her marriage.

Behold me then, gentle reader, seated with my mother on the outside of a stage-coach, with some ten fellow-passengers. The stage-coach of England is quite a different vehicle from the carriage known by that name in America. True, it is drawn by four horses, and it runs on four wheels, but here the likeness ends; instead of being built to carry twelve persons inside, it carries but six, while outside it has seats for twelve. Three or four passengers ride very comfortably behind, in what is called the basket, which is the territory of the guard, as the boot before is of the coachman. All mail coaches, and all others traveling in the night, carry a guard, or an armed man, for the purpose of protecting the coach from the attacks of footpads or highway robbers.

The dullness of our journey was somewhat relieved, after a long season of silence, by the distress of an unfortunate passenger, who, falling asleep, nodded so violently, that his hat, supposing it was receiving notice to quit, very unceremoniously took leave of the skull it covered, and plunged into the mud. The outcry of the poor passenger, who was soon waked by the wind sporting amid his hair, and his unavailing requests to stop the stage, put us all into good humor with ourselves and with each other.

We had another source of relief in the antics of a wild, hair-brained sailor. From spinning yarns, which looked amazingly like new inventions, he would take to dancing on the roof of the coach; at the foot of a hill he would leap off, and then spring up again with the agility of a monkey, to the no small amusement of the passengers. The more I saw of this reckless, thoughtless tar, the more enamored I became with the idea of a sea life; and thus this journey to my mother's new abode was another link in the chain that decided my future destiny in the drama of life. How strangely and imperceptibly do small events tend to unexpected results. A match may fire a city and lay desolate the work of ages; a single leak may sink a bark and carry desolation to a hundred fire-sides—and trifles in the daily scenes of human life, give character to our immortality. We cannot, therefore, too carefully watch the influence of small events, especially on young minds.

At Woodstock, famed in the annals of England as the scene of the loves of King Henry and Rosamond Clifford, we quitted our stage companions, and proceeded on foot to Bladen, two miles distant. Our road lay through Blenheim or Woodstock park, which we entered through the triumphal arch, a spacious portal, erected to the memory of John, Duke of Marlborough, by Sarah, his duchess. On entering the park, which is nearly twelve miles in circumference, one of the most beautiful prospects imaginable disclosed itself. Blenheim Palace, which is among the most magnificent piles of architecture in England, appeared in front; on the left were to be seen a part of the village of Woodstock, and on the right a broad and spacious lake, crossed by a superb bridge;[1] a lofty column on the rising ground, erected in honor of John, Duke of Marlborough, on which is the statue of that noble warrior; a delightful valley, hills, plantations, herds of deer feeding, shady groves and ancient trees, all conspired to render the scene enchantingly beautiful.

Blenheim Palace, or Castle, was built at the public expense, in the reign of Queen Anne, and was given, with its annexed demesnes, in concurrence with the voice of parliament, to John, Duke of Marlborough, as a testimony of royal favor and national gratitude for his successes over the French and Bavarians; particularly for his victory at Blenheim, ort the banks of the Danube, on the 2d of August, 1704.

Crossing the park towards Bladen, we were met by my father-in-law,[2] who received me with a kindness which prepossessed me at once in his favor; he conducted us home, where, to my no small gratification, I met my sister.

My father-in-law appeared to be in comfortable circumstances. He resided in a very neat house, built of stone, shaded by a noble apricot tree, and ornamented with a small but pretty garden. This,

---

[1] Near this bridge is a spring, called Rosamond's Well, where Henry II. is said to have contrived a labyrinth, by which his guilty fair one communicated with the castle.

[2] This form of "step-father" seems not to have been unusual in England 1800-50. Cf. Sam Weller's addressing his father's second wife as "mother-in-law."

together with another similar tenement, was his own property. To add to my satisfaction, I perceived that he was very kind to my mother, and also to myself. She one day expressed a desire to have the cold stone floor of the kitchen removed, and boarded instead; my father, at considerable expense, gratified her wish; this assured me of his regard for her comfort.

With the village itself, I was equally well pleased. Though containing few houses, it was delightfully pleasant. Fine farms, with large flocks of quiet sheep grazing on their hill-sides; expansive fields, surrounded with fragrant hawthorn hedges; and old farmhouses, with their thatched roofs, and massive wheat ricks, met the pleased eye on all sides; while cultivated gardens and numerous wild flowers, especially the modest cowslip and humble violet, scented the air and perfumed the breeze. Thus far, perhaps, Bladen was equal to Wanstead; but in its moral aspects it was inferior. There was far less regard for the Sabbath; less attention to the moral culture of the young, than at the latter place. That blessed institution, which has vivified and renewed the church, which has filled her with the vigorous pulsations of youth—from which, as from some prolific nursery, she has obtained the plants, which now stand on her mountain-tops like the tall cedars of Lebanon—the modest, unassuming Sabbath school was not there. Consequently, the Sabbath was spent in roaming about the fields, in amusements, in visiting, in taking excursions to a place called Ramsden, some seven miles distant. True, there was a parish church, with two clergymen belonging to its altars, but there was service only once every Sunday within its ancient walls. During Lent, however, both priests and people were more religious; the church was better attended; the children were examined as to their knowledge of the church catechism! They were even excited to diligence in committing it to memory by the inducement of reward. A Bible and two prayer books were given to the lads who excelled in answering the questions. At the first Lent examination after my coming to Bladen, the Bible, the highest prize, was awarded to me, and the second year the minister assigned me the task of hearing the others recite— a striking proof of the benefit of Sunday school instruction; it gave me both a moral and mental superiority over all my compeers in the little village of Bladen. This special attention to religion only lasted during the term of Lent; when, with a return to the use of meat, the people returned to the neglect of the Sabbath.

The inhabitants of Bladen were very social in their habits. They held an annual feast, called Bladen feast, to which they invited their friends from other towns; it commenced on Sabbath and continued three days. Eating, drinking, talking, fortune-telling, gambling, occupied three, days of wassail and jollity; after which the visitors returned to their respective towns, and the people to their occupations. The neighboring villages gave similar feasts in their turn. They were occasions of much evil and folly.

My time flew very rapidly and pleasantly away for two or three years, until, like most children, I began to sigh for deliverance from the restraints of home. I had already left school, and for some time, being now about thirteen years of age, had been employed in the pleasure-grounds of Blenheim Palace. This, however, was too tame a business for a lad of my spirits. I had heard tales of the sea from my cousins; my mother had filled my mind with the exploits of my grandfather; my imagination painted a life on the great deep in the most glowing colors; my mind grew uneasy; every day, my ordinary pursuits became more and more irksome, and I was continually talking about going to sea; indeed, I had made myself unhappy by being so discontented.

Little do lads and young men know of the difference between the comfort of a parent's roof and the indifference, unkindness, and trouble they invariably experience, who go out into the world, until they have made the experiment. They paint everything in bright colors; they fancy the future to be all sunshine, all sweets, all flowers, but are sure to be woefully disappointed, when once away from the fireside of their infancy. Let me advise young people, if they wish to escape hardships, to be contented, to remain quietly at home, abiding the openings of Providence, obeying the wishes of their parents, who not only have their best good at heart, but, however they may think to the contrary, actually know what is most for their advantage.

My passion for a seaman's life was not a little increased by a soldier, who was sergeant to a company in Lord Francis Spencer's regiment of cavalry. Seated by my father's hearth-side, this old soldier, who had once been a sailor, would beguile many an evening hour with his endless tale, while I sat listening in rapt attention. My mother, too, heedlessly fanned the flame by her descriptions of the noble appearance of the ships she had seen when at Brighton. Besides this, a footman at Blenheim House used to sing a song called "the poor little sailor boy;" which, although somewhat gloomy in its descriptions, only served to heighten the flame of desire within me, until I could think of nothing else, day or night, but of going to sea.

Finding my desires so strong, my kind-hearted mother mentioned them to Lady Spencer. Just at that time, her brother, Lord William Fitzroy, who was then expecting the command of a frigate, and with whom my departed father had lived as valet, happened to visit Blenheim, previously to going to sea. Anxious to serve my mother, Lady Spencer mentioned me to Lord Fitzroy. He sent for me. Trembling in every joint, I was ushered into his presence. He inquired if I should like to go to sea. "Yes, my lord, I should," was my ready answer. He dismissed me, after some further questionings; but was heard to say, before he left, that he would take me under his care, and see to my future advancement.

These dazzling prospects not only well nigh turned my brain, but decided my parents to send me to sea. To have their son an *officer* in the navy was an unlooked-for honor; and they now entered into my plans and feelings with almost as much ardor as myself. Alas! We were all doomed to learn how little confidence can be placed in the promises of nobles!

Not long after Lord Fitzroy's departure, we received a letter stating the fact of his appointment to his majesty's frigate *Macedonian,* which, being out of dock, was rapidly preparing for sea. This intelligence was the signal for bustle, excitement, preparation, and I know not what. Friends and gossips constantly crowded in to administer their gratuitous advice; some predicting, to my infinite delight, that certainly so smart a boy would make a great man; others wore very grave countenances, and gave certain expressive shrugs of the shoulders, while they told of flogging through the fleet, or of being "seized up" for merely a look or a word; in short, but for a strong conviction in my own breast that this was all said for effect, it is doubtful whether they would not have succeeded in deterring me from my purpose.

At last, after much ado, the long-expected day arrived when I was to bid farewell to home and friends, to venture abroad upon an unknown future. It would only vex the reader by its commonplace character, or I would reveal all the nice little acts of parental, brotherly and neighborly affection which took place. Suffice it to say, that my parting was very much the same as that of all other boys of twelve, when they leave home for the first time—a mixture of hopes and fears, of tears and smiles, of sunshine and cloud.

Attended by my mother and her infant daughter, on the 12th day of July, 1810, I turned my back on the quiet hamlet of Bladen. Henceforth my lot was to be cast amid noise, dissipation, storms and danger. This, however, disturbed my mind but little; brushing away a tear, I leaped gaily on to the outside of the coach, and in a few minutes, enveloped in a cloud of dust, was on my way to London, filled with the one absorbing idea, "I am going to sea! I am going to sea!" Should the reader take the trouble to read the following chapters, he will learn the mishaps, hardships, pleasures and successes that befell me there; and though my narrative may not be filled with the witching tales, and romantic descriptions, that abound in the works of the novelist, it shall at least commend itself to his notice for its truthfulness.

CHAPTER TWO

BEFORE we sought the decks of the *Macedonian* we paid a short visit to Wanstead, where we met with very pleasant reception, very hospitable entertainment, very affectionate adieus. Returning to London, we hired a boat and sailed down the Thames, on whose bosom reposed the commerce of the world, to Gravesend, where we spent the night. The next morning I experienced a new gratification, which was nothing less than being arrayed in a complete suit of sailor apparel; a tarpaulin hat, round blue jacket and wide pantaloons. Never did young knight swell with loftier emotion when donning for the first time his iron dress, than I did when in sea dress I trod the streets of Gravesend. This had always been my highest ambition. The gaudily dressed soldier never had charms for me; but a sailor, how nice he looked! Well, here I stood, at last, in the often coveted dress; it was the first luxury connected with my life at sea. Pity that each successive step had not yielded me equal delight. But it was mine to learn that anticipation and reality were not born twins; that in fact there are scarcely any two existences so essentially different in their characteristics. That I should not lack the means of comfort, my good mother purchased me a chest of clothing, and, as her last token of maternal care, presented me with a Bible, a prayer book, and, strangely inconsistent companions, a pack of cards! Thus equipped, we once more hired a boat and descended the river two miles below Gravesend, where lay the *Macedonian,* in graceful majesty on the sparkling waters.

The first guest we met on board was *disappointment.* From the promises of Lord Fitzroy, we very strangely supposed that he felt my importance nearly as much as did my mother or father. Judge then how we felt, when we learned that no one knew anything in particular about my veritable self; yet, as his Lordship was absent, they said I might remain on board until his return. This was rather a damper on my spirits, but flattering myself that all would be right on his return, I soon rallied again, and, aided by the presence of my mother, passed a very agreeable day.

Towards night, my mother left me; it scarcely need be said, she wept when we parted. What mother would not? She did weep, she strained me to her heart, and impressed affection's purest kiss upon my cheek. How like a dream that moment fled! Now, she held me in her arms; a moment after, she was seated in the light boat and gliding along the turbid Thames, on her homeward way. I leaned over the taffrail and gazed on the departing boat, and when it disappeared, I turned away and wept.

The morning after my arrival, I was put into a "mess." The crew of a man of war is divided into little communities of about eight, called *messes*. These eat and drink together, and are, as it were, so many families. The mess to which I was introduced, was composed of your genuine, weather-beaten, old tars. But for one of its members, it would have suited me very well; this one, a real gruff old "bull-dog," named Hudson, took into his head to hate me at first sight. He treated me with so much abuse and unkindness, that my messmates soon advised me to change my mess, a privilege which is wisely allowed, and which tends very much to the good fellowship of a ship's crew; for if there are disagreeable men among them, they can in this way be got rid of; it is no infrequent case to find a few, who have been spurned from all the messes in the ship, obliged to mess by themselves.

This unkindness from the brutal Hudson rather chilled my enthusiasm. The crew, too, by some means had an impression that my mother had brought me on board to get rid of me, and therefore bestowed their bitterest curses on her in the most profuse manner imaginable. Swearing I had heard before, but never such as I heard there. Nor was this all; in performing the work assigned me, which consisted in helping the seamen take in provisions, powder, shot, etc., I felt the insults and tyranny of the midshipmen. These little minions of power ordered and drove me round like a dog, nor did I and the other boys dare interpose a word. They were *officers;* their word was our law, and woe betide the presumptuous boy that dared refuse implicit obedience.

These things reminded me of what had been said to me of the hardships of sea life in a man of war. I began to wish myself back in my father's house at Bladen. This, however, was impossible, and to add to my discouragement they told me I was entered on the ship's books for life. Dreary prospect! I felt more than half disposed, as I went to my tasks, to use the language of the Irishman, as sung by my shipmates. Tempted and beguiled while intoxicated, he had enlisted for a soldier, but found the sergeant at the *recruiting office* and the sergeant on the *drill-field* very different personages. He is hence made to say,

> It was early next morning to drill I was sent,
> And its och to my soul! I began to lament;
> Cannot you be aisy and let me alone?
> Don't you see I've got arms, legs, and feet of my own?

But although somewhat grieved with my first experience of sailor life, I secretly struggled against my feelings, and with the most philosophic desperation resolved to make the best of my condition. We were kept busily at work every day until the ship's stores were all on board, and our frigate was ready for sea. Then two hundred more men, drafted from receiving ships, came on board, to complete the number of our crew, which, after this addition, numbered full three hundred men. The jocularity, pleasantry, humor and good feeling that now prevailed on board our frigate, somewhat softened the unpleasantness of my lot, and cultivated a feeling of reconciliation to my circumstances. Various little friendships, which sprang up between me and my shipmates, threw a gleam of gladness across my path; a habit of attention, respect and obedience in a short time secured me universal good will. I began to be tolerably satisfied.

Many boys complain of ill usage at sea. I know they are subjected to it in many instances; yet, in most cases, they owe it to their own boldness. A boy on shipboard, who is habitually saucy, will be kicked and cuffed by all with whom he has to do; he will be made miserable. The reason is, I imagine, that sailors, being treated as inferiors themselves, love to find opportunity to act the *superior* over some one. They do this over the boys, and if they find a saucy, insolent one, they show him no mercy. Permit me, then, to advise boys who go to sea, to be civil and obliging to all; they will be amply repaid for the effort it may cost them to make the trial, especially if they gain the reputation, as I did, of being among the best boys in the ship.

A vessel of war contains a little community of human beings, isolated, for the time being, from the rest of mankind. This community is governed by laws peculiar to itself; it is arranged and divided in a manner suitable to its circumstances. Hence, when its members first come together, each one is assigned his respective station and duty. For every task, from getting up the anchor to unbending the sails, aloft and below, at the mess-tub or in the hammock, each task has its man, and each man his place. A ship contains a set of human machinery, in which every man is a wheel, a band, or a crank, all moving with wonderful regularity and precision to the will of its machinist—the all-powerful captain.

The men are distributed in all parts of the vessel; those in the tops are called fore-top-men, main-top-men, and mizzen-top-men, with two captains to each top, one for each watch. These top-men have to loose, take in, reef and furl the sails aloft, such as the top-gallant sails, top-sails, top-gallant royal, and top-sail studding-sails. Others are called forecastle men, waisters, and the after-guard; these have to loose, tend, and furl the courses, that is, the fore-sail, the main-sail and lower studding-sails; they also have to set the jib, flying-jib, and spanker; the after-guard have a special charge to coil up all ropes in the after part of the ship. Others are called *scavengers;* these, as their not very attractive name imports, have to sweep and pick up the dirt that may chance to gather through the day, and throw it overboard. Then come the boys, who are mostly employed as servants to the officers. Our captain had a steward and a boy; these acted as his domestic servants in his large and stately cabin, which, to meet the ideas of landsmen, may be called his house. The lieutenants, purser, surgeon, and sailing-master, had each a boy; they, together with the two lieutenants of marines, who were waited upon by two marines, form what is called the ward-room officers. The ward-room is a large cabin, (I mean large for a ship, of course,) below the captain's, where they all mess together; aft of this cabin is a smaller one, which serves as a species of store-room. Besides these accommodations, every ward-room officer has his state-room, containing his cot, wash-stand, writing-desk, clothes, etc. The gunner, boatswain, and some others, are also allowed a boy; and a man and boy are appointed to be the servants of a certain number of midshipmen.

Another arrangement is that of forming the ship's company into watches. The captain, first lieutenant, surgeon, purser, boatswain, gunner, carpenter, armorer, together with the stewards and boys, are excused from belonging to them, but are liable to be called out to take in sail; some of the last mentioned are called *idlers.* All others are in watches, called the larboard and starboard watches.

Stations are also assigned at the guns, to the whole crew. When at sea, the drummer beats to quarters every night. This beat, by which the men are summoned to quarters, is a regular tune.

I have often heard the words sung which belong to it; this is the chorus:

> Hearts of oak are our ships, jolly tars are our men,
> We always are ready, steady, boys, steady,
> To fight and to conquer again and again.

At the roll of this evening drum, all hands hurry to the guns. Eight men and a boy are stationed at each gun, one of whom is captain of the gun, another sponges and loads it, the rest take hold of the side tackle-falls, to run the gun in and out; while the boy is employed in handing the cartridges, for which he is honored with the singularly euphonious cognomen of powder-monkey.

Besides these arrangements among the men, there are from thirty to forty marines to be disposed of. These do duty as sentries at the captain's cabin, the ward-room, and at the galley during the time of cooking. They are also stationed at the large guns at night, as far as their numbers run. When a ship is in action, and small arms can be brought to bear on the enemy, they are stationed on the spar-deck; they are also expected to assist in boarding, in conjunction with several seamen from each gun, who are armed with pistols and pikes, and called boarders.

The great disparity of numbers between the crew of a merchant ship and that of a man of war, occasions a difference in their internal arrangements and mode of life, scarcely conceivable by those who have not seen both. This is seen throughout, from the act of rousing the hands in the morning to that of taking in sail. In the merchantman, the watch below is called up by a few strokes of the handspike on the forecastle; in the man of war, by the boatswain and his mates. The boatswain is a petty officer, of considerable importance in his way; he and his mates carry a small silver whistle or pipe, suspended from the neck by a small cord. He receives word from the officer of the watch to call the hands up. You immediately hear a sharp, shrill whistle; this is succeeded by another and another from his mates. Then follows his hoarse, rough cry of "All hands ahoy!" which is forthwith repeated by his mates. Scarcely has this sound died upon the ear, before the cry of "Up all hammocks ahoy!" succeeds it, to be repeated in like manner. As the first tones of the whistle penetrate between decks, signs of life make their appearance. Rough, uncouth forms are seen tumbling out of their hammocks on all sides, and before its last sounds have died upon the air, the whole company of sleepers are hurriedly preparing for the duties of the day. No delay is permitted, for as soon as the before-mentioned officers have uttered their imperative commands, they run below, each armed with a rope's end, with which they belabor the shoulders of any luckless wight upon whose eyes sleep yet hangs heavily, or whose slow-moving limbs show him to be but half awake.

With a rapidity which would surprise a landsman, the crew dress themselves, lash their hammocks and carry them on deck, where they are stowed for the day. There is system even in this arrangement; every hammock has its appropriate place. Below, the beams are all marked, each hammock is marked with a corresponding number, and in the darkest night, a sailor will go unhesitatingly to his own hammock. They are also kept exceeding clean. Every man is provided with two, so that while he is scrubbing and cleaning one, he may have another to use. Nothing but such precautions could enable so many men to live in so small a space.

A similar rapidity attends the performance of every duty. The word of command is given in the same manner, and its prompt obedience enforced by the same unceremonious rope's-end. To skulk is therefore next to impossible; the least tardiness is rebuked by the cry of "Hurrah my hearty! Bear a hand! Heave along! Heave along!" This system of driving is far from being agreeable; it perpetually reminds you of your want of liberty; it makes you feel, sometimes, as if the hardest crust, the most ragged garments, with the freedom of your own native hills, would be preferable to John Bull's "beef and duff," joined as it is with the rope's-end of the driving boatswain.

We had one poor fellow, an Irishman, named Billy Garvy, who felt very uneasy and unhappy. He was the victim of that mortifying system of impressment, prevalent in Great Britain in time of war. He came on board perfectly unacquainted with the mysteries of sea life.. One of his first inquiries was, where he should find his bed, supposing they slept on shipboard on beds the same as on shore. His messmates, with true sailor roguishness, sent him to the boatswain. "And where shall I find a bed, sir?" asked he of this rugged son of the ocean.

The boatswain looked at him very contemptuously for a moment, then, rolling his lump of tobacco into another apartment of his ample mouth, replied,

"Have you got a knife?"

"Yes, sir."

"Well, stick it into the softest plank in the ship, and take that for a bed!"

Poor fellow! what was sport for others was pain to him. He had been used to kind treatment at home. After he had received his hammock, when turning out in the morning, with the boatswain's mates at his heels, he used to exclaim, "When I was at home, I would walk in my father's garden in the morning, until the maid would come and say, 'William, will you come to your ta, or your coffee ta, or your chocolarata?' But, oh! the case is altered now; it's nothing but bear a hand, lash and carry. Oh, dear! "

I confess that Billy Garvy was not the only one who contrasted the present with the past, or who found the balance to be greatly in favor of the former. I often looked back to the village of Bladen, and thought how preferable would be the bright hearth-side and pleasant voices of that quiet home, to the profane, rough, uncomfortable life we led on shipboard. As these reflections were anything but pleasurable, I banished them as quickly as possible, with a determination to be as happy as I could in my station of servant to the surgeon of His Britannic Majesty's frigate *Macedonian:* a resolution which I commend to all lads, who, like me, are foolish enough to quit the quiet scenes of a native village, for the noisy, profane atmosphere of a man of war.

As our fare was novel and so different from shore living, it was some time before I could get fully reconciled to it: it was composed of hard sea biscuit, fresh beef while in port, but salt pork and salt beef at sea, pea soup and burgoo. Burgoo, or, as it was sportively called, skillagallee, was oatmeal boiled in water to the consistency of hasty pudding. Sometimes we had cocoa instead of burgoo. Once a week we had flour and raisins served out, with which we made "duff" or pudding. To prepare these articles, each mess had its cook, who drew the provisions, made the duff, washed the mess kids, etc. He also drew the grog for the mess, which consisted of a gill of rum mixed with two gills of water for each man. This was served out at noon every day: at four o'clock, P.M., each man received half a pint of wine. The boys only drew half this quantity, but were allowed pay for the remainder, a regulation which could have been profitably applied to the whole supply of grog and wine for both boys and men. But those were not days in which Temperance triumphed as she does now; though, I believe, the British navy has not yet ceased to dispense the "drink that's in the drunkard's bowl" to her seamen.

Shortly after our captain came on board, his servant died somewhat suddenly, so that I had an early opportunity of seeing how sailors are disposed of in this sad hour. The corpse was laid out on the grating, covered with a flag; as we were yet in the river, the body was taken on shore and buried, without the beautiful burial-service of the church of England being read at his grave—a ceremony which is not omitted at the interment of the veriest pauper in that country.

I have purposely dwelt on these particulars, that the reader may feel himself initiated at once into the secrets of man-of-war usages. He has doubtless seen ships of war with their trim rigging and frowning ports, and his heart has swelled with pride as he has gazed upon these floating cities—the representatives of his nation's character in foreign countries: to their internal arrangements, however, he has been a stranger. I have endeavored to introduce him into the interior: a desire to make him feel at home there, is my apology for dwelling so long on these descriptions.

After various delays, we were at last ready for sea and under sailing orders. The tide and wind were both propitious; then came the long-expected cry of the boatswain, "All hands up anchor ahoy!" The crew manned the capstan in a trice, and running round to the tune of a lively air played by the filer, the huge anchor rapidly left the mud of the Thames, and hung at the bows of our taut frigate. Then came the cry of "All hands make sail ahoy!" As if by magic, she was immediately covered with canvas; the favoring breeze at once filled our sails, and the form that had lain for weeks inert and motionless on the waters, now bounded along the waves like a thing of life. Rapidly we ran down the Channel, and before we had well got under weigh came to an anchor again at Spithead, under shelter of the garden of England—the Isle of Wight.

Short as was the period between weighing anchor off Gravesend and our arrival at Spithead, it gave opportunity for one of those occurrences which are a disgrace to the naval service of any nation, and a degradation to our common humanity, which the public opinion of the civilized world should frown out of existence: I allude to the brutal practice of flogging.

A poor fellow had fallen into the very sailor-like offense of getting drunk. For this the captain sentenced him to the punishment of four dozen lashes. He was first placed in *irons* all night: the irons used for this purpose were shackles fitting round the ankles, through the ends of which was passed an iron bar some ten or twelve feet in length: it was thus long because it was no unfrequent case for half a dozen men to be ironed at once. A padlock at the end of the bar held the prisoner securely. Thus placed in "duress vile," he was guarded by a marine until the captain bade the first lieutenant prepare the hands to witness the punishment. Upon this the lieutenant transmitted the order to the master at arms. He then ordered the grating or hatch full of square holes to be rigged: it was placed accordingly between the main and spar decks, not far from the mainmast.

While these preparations were going on, the officers were dressing themselves in full uniform and arming themselves with their dirks: the prisoner's messmates carried him his best clothes, to make him appear in as decent a manner as possible. This is always done, in the hope of moving the feelings of the captain favorably towards the prisoner.

This done, the hoarse, dreaded cry of "All hands ahoy to witness punishment!" from the lips of the boatswain, peals along the ship as mournfully as the notes of a funeral knell. At this signal the officers muster on the spar deck, the men on the main deck. Next came the prisoner; guarded by a marine on one side and the master at arms on the other, he was marched up to the grating. His back was made bare and his shirt laid loosely upon his back; the two quartermasters proceeded to seize him up; that is, they tied his hands and feet with spun-yarns, called the seizings, to the grating. The boatswain's mates, whose office it is to flog on board a man of war, stood ready with their dreadful weapon of punishment, the cat-o'-nine-tails. This instrument of torture was composed of nine cords, a quarter of an inch round and about two feet long, the ends whipped with fine twine. To these cords was affixed a stock, two feet in length, covered with red baize. The reader may be sure that it is a most formidable instrument in the hands of a strong, skillful man. Indeed, any man who should whip his horse with it would commit an outrage on humanity, which the moral feeling of any community would not tolerate; he would be prosecuted for cruelty; yet it is used to whip men on board ships of war!

The boatswain's mate is ready, with coat off and whip in hand. The captain gives the word. Carefully spreading the cords with the fingers of his left hand, the executioner throws the cat over his right shoulder; it is brought down upon the now uncovered herculean shoulders of the max. His flesh creeps—it reddens as if blushing at the indignity; the sufferer groans; lash follows lash, until the first mate, wearied with the cruel employment, gives place to a second. Now two dozen of these dreadful lashes have been inflicted: the lacerated back looks inhuman; it resembles roasted meat burnt nearly black before a scorching fire; yet still the lashes fall; the captain continues merciless. Vain are the cries and prayers of the wretched man. "I would not forgive the Saviour," was the blasphemous reply of one of these naval demi-gods, or rather demi-fiends, to a plea for mercy. The executioners keep on. Four dozen strokes have cut up his flesh and robbed him of all self-respect; there he hangs, a pitied, self-despised, groaning, bleeding wretch; and now the captain cries, forbear! His shirt is thrown over his shoulders; the seizings are loosed; he is led away, staining his path with red drops of blood, and the hands, "piped down" by the boatswain, sullenly return to their duties.

Such was the scene witnessed on board the *Macedonian,* on the passage from London to Spithead; such, substantially, is every punishment scene at sea; only carried, sometimes, to a greater length of severity. Sad and sorrowful were my feelings on witnessing it; thoughts of the friendly warnings of my old acquaintance filled my mind, and I inwardly wished myself once more under the friendly roof of my father, at Bladen. Vain wish! I should have believed the warning voice when it was given. Believe me, young man, you will often breathe that wish, if ever you wander from a father's house.

Flogging in the navy is more severe than in the army, though it is too bad to be tolerated there, or indeed anywhere. Other modes of punishment might be successfully substituted, which would deter from misconduct, without destroying the self-respect of the man. I hope the day will come, when a captain will no more be allowed to use the "cat" than he is now to use poison. It should be an interdicted weapon.

Though I have spoken severely of the officers of the navy, let it not be thought that the whole class of naval officers are lost to the finer feelings of humanity. There are many humane, considerate men among them, who deserve our highest respect. This was the case with the first lieutenant of the *Macedonian,* Mr. Scott. He abhorred flogging. Once, when a poor marine was under sentence, he plead hard and successfully with the captain for his respite. This was a great victory; for the captain had a profound hatred of marines. The poor soldier was extremely grateful for his intercession, and would do anything for him to show his sense of the obligation; indeed, the sailors, in their odd way, showed their preference for him by describing him as a man who had a soul to be saved, and who ought to go to heaven; while of the captain, they whispered that if he did not go to perdition, "the devil would be cheated of his due." These are, in a manner, proverbial expressions of like and dislike, on board a British man of war.

One of the effects of this exhibition of cruelty was seen during the short time we lay at Spithead. The two boys, who were servants to the first and second lieutenants, conceiving a special dislike to the idea of being flogged, took it into their heads to run away. Being sent on shore, they shaped their course for the country. It was well for them that they were not re-taken.

Our frigate had orders to convey between two and three hundred troops from Portsmouth to Lisbon, to assist the Portuguese against the French. The soldiers were stowed on the main decks, with very few conveniences for the voyage; their officers messed and berthed in the ward-room. Having taken them on board, we again weighed anchor, and were soon careering before the breeze on our way to Lisbon.

As usual, we who were landsmen had our share of that merciless, nondescript, hateful, stultifying disease, yclept sea-sickness; as usual, we wished the foolish wish that we had never come to sea; as usual, we got over it, and laughed at ourselves for our sea-sick follies. Our good ship paid little attention, however, to our feelings; she kept along on her bounding way, and, after a week at sea, we were greeted with the pleasant cry of "Land ho!" from the mast-head. As it was now near night, we lay off and on until morning; at day-break we fired a gun for a pilot. The wind 'being nearly dead ahead, we had to beat about nearly all day. Towards night it became fair, and we ascended the Tagus. This river is about nine miles wide at its mouth, and is four hundred and fifty miles in length; it has a very rapid current, with steep, fertile banks. Aided by a fine breeze, we ascended it in splendid style, passed a half-moon battery, then shot past Belem Castle into the port of Lisbon, about ten miles from its mouth. Here we found a spacious harbor, filled with shipping. Besides numerous merchantmen, there were two ships of a hundred guns, several seventy-fours, frigates and sloops of war, with a large number of transports; all designed for the defense of Lisbon against the French.

Lisbon has a fine appearance from the harbor. A stranger, after a long sea-voyage, while standing on the deck of his vessel, and gazing on its battlements and towers, might fancy it to be a terrestrial paradise; but, on landing, his admiration would certainly sink below zero, as he plodded his way, beset by saucy beggars at almost every step, through its narrow, filthy streets. Such, at least, was my impression, as I perambulated the city. Among other things, I noticed a great variety of churches and convents, which furnished swarms of plump, good-natured friars, under whose spiritual domination the good people of Lisbon were content to rest. I also counted thirteen large squares. One of them contained a huge black horse, standing in its centre, with the figure of a man upon his back, both much larger than life. What this monument represented, I did not learn. That square is denominated Black Horse Square.

On the day after our arrival, the *Macedonian* was the scene of considerable bustle. The troops, who seemed to forget their proximity to a field of carnage, in the delight they felt at escaping from the confinement on shipboard, were landed; several boats' crews were also sent up the river to assist in the defense of the place.

While we lay here, our ship was well supplied with fruits from the shore. Large bunches of delicious grapes, abundance of sweet oranges, water-melons, chestnuts, and also a bountiful supply of gigantic onions, of peculiar flavor, enabled our crew to gratify their palates in true English style. Poor fellows! they feasted, laughed, and joked, as if the future had nothing to develop but fairy scenes of unmixed delight. Little thought, indeed, does your true tar take of the morrow.

Amid these feastings, however, there rose something to trouble Macbeth, in the shape of an order from the admiral to prepare for a cruise. This was peremptory—for a cruise, therefore, we prepared. Our boats' crews came on board; the officers stored their larder with the means of gustatory gratifications; and we stood out to sea again.

The port of Corunna, in Spain, was the next place at which we anchored. While lying in this spacious and safe harbor, our little world was thrown into temporary confusion by the loss of the wardroom steward, Mr. Sanders. This man could speak in the Spanish tongue; he had accumulated a considerable sum of money by long service, prize money, and an economy little known among sailors. For some cause or other he had become dissatisfied; so, one day, he engaged a Spaniard to run his boat under the stern of our frigate; dropping from one of the stern ports into the boat, unperceived by the officers, the wily Spaniards covered him with their loose garments and sails, and then conveyed him to the shore. This was running a great risk; for had he been detected in the act, or taken afterwards, he would have felt the cruel strokes of the lash. Fortunately for himself, he escaped without detection.

From Corunna, we returned to Lisbon, where, at the cheerful cry of "All hands bring the ship to an anchor, ahoy!" we once more placed our frigate, taut and trim, under the battlements of the city.

As servant to the surgeon, it was one part of my duty to perform the task of carrying his clothes to be washed. As great attention to cleanliness, in frequently changing their linen, is observed among naval officers, a good washerwoman is considered quite a desideratum. In attending to this matter for my master, I had frequent opportunities to go on shore. This gave me some means of observation. On one of my visits to our pretty laundress, I saw several Portuguese running along, gesticulating and talking with great earnestness. Being ignorant of their language, my washerwoman, who spoke good English, told me that a man had been stabbed, in consequence of some ground for jealousy, afforded by the conduct of the deceased. Hastening to the spot, I saw the wounded man, stretched out on a bed, with two gaping wounds in his side, the long knife, the instrument of the deed, lying by his side. The poor sufferer soon died. What was done to the murderer, I could not discover.

Though very passionate, and addicted to the use of the knife, for the purpose of taking summary vengeance, the Portuguese are nevertheless arrant cowards. Indeed, it is a question by no means settled, whether all classes of men, in any country, who fly to cold steel or to fire-arms in every petty quarrel, are not cowards at heart. We had an evidence of Portuguese cowardice in an affray which occurred between some of the citizens of Lisbon and a party of our marines. Six of the latter, ignorant of the palace or municipal regulations, wandered into the queen's gardens. Some twenty of the Portuguese, on witnessing this bold intrusion on the privacy of the queen, rushed upon them with long knives. The marines, though so inferior in number, faced about with their bayonets, and, after much cursing and chattering, their enemies, considering perhaps that the better part of valor is discretion, took to their heels, leaving the six marines masters of a bloodless field. These recontres were quite common between them and our men; the result, though sometimes more serious, was uniformly the same.

As an illustration of the manners of this people, I cannot forbear the insertion of another fact. I was one day walking leisurely along the streets, quite at my ease, when the gathering of a noisy multitude arrested my attention. Looking up, I was shocked at seeing a human head, with a pair of hands beneath it, nailed to a pole! They had just been taken from the body of a barber, who, when in the act of shaving a gentleman, was seized with a sudden desire to possess a beautiful watch, which glittered in his pocket; to gain this brilliant bauble, the wretched man cut his victim's throat. He was arrested, his hands were cut off, then his head, and both were fastened to the pole as I have described them. Upon inquiry, I ascertained that this was the ordinary method of punishing murder in Portugal; a striking evidence that civilization had not fully completed its great work among them. Civilization humanizes the feelings of society, throwing a veil of refinement and mercy over even the sterner acts of justice; at any rate, it never tolerates such barbarism as I saw at Lisbon.

While in port we experienced a change of officers by no means agreeable to the crew. Mr. Scott, our first lieutenant, an amiable man, decidedly hostile to the practice of flogging, left us; for what cause, we could not ascertain. His successor, Mr. Hope, though bearing a very pleasant name, was an entirely different person, in manners and conduct, from his predecessor. He was harsh, severe, and fond of seeing the men flogged. Of course, floggings became more frequent than before; for, although a lieutenant cannot flog upon his own authority, yet, such is the influence he exerts over a captain, that he has the utmost opportunity to gratify a thirst for punishment. It may appear strange to the reader that any gentleman—and all officers of the navy consider themselves *gentlemen* —should possess such a thirst; yet such was the case with Mr. Hope. Nor was his a solitary example; many a man, who, on shore, in presence of ladies of fashion, appeared too gentle to harm an enemy, too kind to injure an insect, was strangely metamorphosed into a genuine unprincipled tyrant, upon assuming command in a man of war.

We had already witnessed a number of punishments, especially at sea: in port, the officers were more condescending, lest their men should desert; but at sea, when this was impossible, they flogged without mercy. Cases of offense which occurred while in the harbor, were looked up; sometimes a half dozen were flogged at once; every man trembled lest he should be a victim; the ship's crew were made wretched; a sword seemed impending over every head. Who, in such a case, could be happy? Not even a sailor, with all his habitual thoughtlessness. Yet it is said we must flog, to maintain discipline among sailors. Pshaw! Flogging may be needful to awe a slave writhing under a sense of unmerited wrong, but never should a lash fall on a freeman's back, especially if he holds the safety and honor of his country in his keeping.

Poor old Bob Hammond! Never was man more reckless than this honest-hearted Irishman; never was sailor more courageous under punishment. For being drunk he received four dozen lashes; he bore the infliction with profound silence, uttering neither groan nor sigh; neither casting one imploring look at his tormentors. On being taken down, he applied himself most lustily to his bottle, and before night was drunk again. Rushing to the quarter deck, with a madness peculiar to a frenzied drunkard, he ran up against the captain with such force that he nearly knocked him down. With a boldness that seemed to strike the great man dumb, Bob hiccuped and said,

"Halloo, Billy, my boy, is that you? You are young and foolish; just fit for the launch. You are like a young lion—all your sorrows are to come."

The captain was excessively proud; even his officers scarcely dared walk the quarter deck on the same side with him. He never allowed himself to be addressed but by his title of "my Lord." Should a sailor, through design or forgetfulness, reply to a command, "Yes, sir," the lordly man would look at him with a glance full of dignity, and sternly reply, "What, sir?" This, of course, would put the offender in mind to correct himself by saying, "Yes, my *Lord*." Judge then of his surprise, indignation, nay, of his lordly horror, when poor old drunken Bob Hammond called him "Billy, my boy!" Doubtless it stirred up his nobility within him, for, with a voice of thunder, he exclaimed, "Put this man in irons!" It was done. The next morning, his back yet sore, poor Bob received five dozen more strokes of the hated cat-o'-nine-tails. Most heroically was it borne. No sound escaped him; the most profound silence was observed by all, broken only by the dead sound of the whip, as it fell every few moments on the wounded back. The scene was sickening in the extreme. Let me throw a veil over its details, simply remarking that it is questionable which of the two appears to the best advantage; poor drunken Bob, suffering degrading torture with heroic firmness, or my Lord Fitzroy, gloating on the scene with the appetite of a vulture! Let the reader decide for himself.

These statements may at first sight appear incredible. It may be asked how a man could endure whippings which would destroy an ox or a horse. This is a very natural question, and but for the consciousness I feel of being supported in my statements by the universal testimony of old men-of-war's-men, I should hesitate to publish them. The *worst* species of this odious torture, however, remains to be described—flogging through the fleet.

This punishment is never inflicted without due trial and sentence by a court-martial, for some aggravated offense. After the offender is thus sentenced, and the day arrives appointed by his judges for its execution, the unhappy wretch is conducted into the ship's launch—a large boat—which has been previously rigged up with poles and grating, to which he is seized up; he is attended by the ship's surgeon, whose duty it is to decide when the power of nature's endurance has been taxed to its utmost. A boat from every ship in the fleet is also present, each carrying one or two officers and two marines fully armed. These boats are connected by tow lines to the launch.

These preparations made, the crew of the victim's ship are ordered to man the rigging, while the boatswain commences the tragedy. When he has administered one, two or three dozen lashes, according to the number of ships in the fleet, the prisoner's shirt is thrown over his gory back; the boatswain returns on board, the hands are piped down, the drummer beats a mournful melody, called the rogue's march, and the melancholy procession moves on. Arriving at the side of another ship, the brutal scene is repeated, until every crew in the fleet has witnessed it, and from one to three hundred lashes have lacerated the back of the broken-spirited tar to a bleeding pulp. He is then placed under the surgeon's care, to be fitted for duty—*a ruined man*—broken in spirit! all sense of self-respect gone, forever gone! If he survive, it is only to be like his own brave bark, when winds and waves conspire to dash her on the pitiless strand, a wretched, hopeless wreck; a living, walking shadow of his former self. A shameful blot! A most foul and disgraceful stain on the humanity of England! How long before this worse than barbarism will disappear before the mild influences of civilization and Christianity?

No plea of necessity can be successfully urged in behalf of whipping men; for, if subordination or faithful adhesion to orders is expected to follow such terrible examples, I know, from my acquaintance with the sufferers themselves, that the expectation is vain. One of two results always follows. The victim either lives on, a lone, dark-minded, broken-spirited man, despising himself and hating every one, because he thinks every one hates him; or he lives with one fearful, unyielding purpose; a purpose on which he

feeds and nourishes his galled mind, as food affords life and en-
ergy to his physical constitution—that purpose is revenge. I have
heard them swear—and the wild flashing eye, the darkly frowning
brow, told how firm was that intent—that if ever they should be in
battle, they would shoot their officers. I have seen them rejoice
over the misfortunes of their persecutors, but more especially at
their death. That it has frequently led to mutiny, is well verified. I
have known such severity to result in actual murder. While we lay
at Lisbon, a sergeant of marines, on board a seventy-four, made
himself obnoxious by repeated acts of tyranny. Two marines determined upon his death. One night, unperceived by any, they
seized him, hurried him to the gangway, and pitched him overboard. The tide was running strong; the man was drowned! But for
themselves his fate would have remained a secret until the great
day of judgment; it was discovered by an officer, who accidentally
overheard them congratulating each other on their achievement.
He betrayed them. A court-martial sentenced them. They were
placed on deck with halters on their necks. Two guns were fired,
and, when the smoke cleared away, two men were seen dangling
from the foreyard-arm. Only one day previous, a letter had
brought a discharge from the service for one of them. Poor fellow!
it came too late. He was fated to a summary discharge from all
service, in a manner appalling and repulsive to every finer human
feeling.

Such are the actual consequences of severity of discipline on
board men of war. Punishment leads to revenge; revenge to punishment. What is intended to cure, only aggravates the disease; the
evil enlarges under the remedy; *voluntary* subordination ceases;
gloom overspreads the crew; fear fills the breasts of the officers;
the ship becomes a miniature of the house of fiends. While, on the
other hand, mild regulations, enforced without an appeal to brute
force, are easily carried into operation. The sailor has a warm
heart; show him personal kindness, treat him as a man, he will
then be a man; he will do anything for a *kind* officer. He will peril
his life for him; nay, he will cheerfully rush between him and danger. This was done at Tripoli, when the brave James[1] offered his
own arm to receive the fell stroke of a Turkish scimitar, aimed at
the life of the bold Decatur, on board the frigate *Philadelphia*. Let
naval officers, let all ship-masters, once fairly test the effect of kind
treatment, and I am sure they will never desire to return to sever-

[1] See: Brady, C.T., Reuben James a hero of the forecastle, New York : D.
Appleton and Company, 1906

ity; unless, indeed, they are tyrants at heart, in which case, the sooner they lose their commands the better for their country; for no tyrant is truly brave or trustworthy. Cowardice and meanness lie curled up in the heart of every tyrant. He is too despicable, too unsafe to be trusted with the responsibilities of a naval command. Such, at least, is the opinion of an old sailor.

One of the greatest enemies to order and happiness in ships of war is drunkenness. To be drunk is considered by almost every sailor as the *acme* of sensual bliss; while many fancy that swearing and drinking are necessary accomplishments in a genuine man-of-war's-man. Hence it almost universally prevails. In our ship the men would get drunk, in defiance of every restriction. Were it not for the moral and physical ruin which follows its use, one might laugh at the various contrivances adopted to elude the vigilance of officers in their efforts to procure rum. Some of our men who belonged to the boats' crews provided themselves with bladders; if left ashore by their officers a few moments, they would slip into the first grocery, fill their bladders, and return with the spoil. Once by the ship's side, the favorable moment was seized to pass the interdicted bladders into the port-holes, to some watchful shipmate, by whom it was carefully secreted, to be drunk at the first opportunity. The liberty to go on shore, which is always granted while in port, was sure to be abused for drunken purposes. The Sabbath was also a day of sensuality. True, we sometimes had the semblance of religious services, when the men were summoned aft to hear the captain read the morning service from the church prayer-book; but usually it was observed more as a day of revelry than of worship. But at Christmas our ship presented a scene such as I had never imagined. The men were permitted to have their "full swing." Drunkenness ruled the ship. Nearly every man, with most of the officers, was in a state of beastly intoxication at night. Here, some were fighting, but were so insensibly drunk, they hardly knew whether they struck the guns or their opponents; yonder, a party were singing libidinous or bacchanalian songs, while all were laughing, cursing, swearing or hallooing; confusion reigned in glorious triumph; it was the very chaos of humanity. Had we been at sea, a sudden gale of wind must have proved our destruction; had we been exposed to a sudden attack from an enemy's vessel, we should have fallen an easy prey to the victor; just as the poor Hessians, at Trenton, fell before the well-timed blow of the sage Washington, during the war of the revolution.

Of all places, the labors of temperance men are most needed among sailors; and I am glad to know that much has been accomplished among them already. From what I *know* of the sufferings and difficulties growing out of intemperance at sea, I most heartily desire to see a temperance flag floating at the mast-head of every ship in the world. When this is seen, sailors will be a happier class than ever they have yet been, from the time when the cautious Phoenicians crept timidly round the shores of the Mediterranean, to the present day of bold and fearless navigation.

CHAPTER THREE

SHORTLY after the Christmas debauch, mentioned in the preceding chapter, news was brought to the admiral that nine French frigates were cruising on the Spanish coast: immediately, all was excitement, bustle, preparation through the fleet. The *Hannibal* and *Northumberland,* both seventy-four gun ships, the *Caesar* of eighty guns, called by the sailors the Old Bull-dog, a gun brig, and some others, I forget the names, and the *Macedonian,* were ordered to sail in pursuit of the French. This formidable force dropped down the river, every man composing it eagerly desiring to meet the enemy. The enterprise however, was unsuccessful; after cruising in vain for several days, the admiral signaled the fleet to return. Before reaching port we fell in with a Scotch ship from Greenock, in a most perilous condition; her masts and rudder were gone, while her numerous leaks were fast gaining on the labors of the already exhausted crew at the pumps. Finding it utterly impossible to save the vessel, we took off the crew; and thus our cruise, though defeated in its main design, proved the means of rescuing several poor wretches from a watery grave. It is a question worthy of consideration, whether this was not a really higher result than if we had found and beaten the French, and had returned in a crippled state, leaving some hundreds killed and wounded. Humanity would answer, yea.

So far as the effects of this cruise concerned our own little frigate, they were really quite serious. We were reefing topsails one night, at sea, when the sailing-master, Mr. Lewis, in a fit of ill-humor, threatened to flog some of the men. The captain overheard him. Feeling himself hurt by this assumption of his own prerogative, he told Mr. Lewis that he was captain in the ship, and it was his business to flog the men. Sharp words followed; the captain was exasperated; he ordered the sailing-master to be put in irons. Here, however, he exceeded his own power, for, though he might place the common sailor in irons, he might not do so by an officer with impunity. Accordingly, when we reached Lisbon, a court-martial sat on the case, which resulted in their both being broken or cashiered.

This was a hard blow for Lord Fitzroy, and he obviously felt it most keenly. It also cut off my expectations of being elevated to the quarter deck; for, although I had never received any direct encouragement from his Lordship, yet I had always nourished the hope that ultimately he would keep the promise he made to my mother, and do something for my advancement. Now, however, my hopes were destroyed. I was doomed to the forecastle for life.

Lord Fitzroy was succeeded by Captain Carson. He however, was soon removed to make way for Captain Waldegrave, who proved to be far more severe than Fitzroy. He and Lieutenant Hope were kindred spirits: cruelty seemed to be their delight, for at the presence of culprits tied to the gratings, a gleam of savage animation stole over their faces. Punishment was now an almost every-day scene; even the boys were not permitted to escape. A lad was appointed boatswain over them, and they were consigned to the care of Mr. Hope, who took especial delight in seeing them flogged. What a mean, dastardly spirit for a British officer! How utterly contemptible he appears engaged in whipping a few helpless sailor boys! Yet thus he did constantly appear, causing them to be flogged for every trifling offense. One poor little fellow, unable to tolerate the thought of the lash, hid himself in the cable tier for several days. He was discovered, only to be most shamefully punished.

These severities filled our crew with discouragement. A sailor dreads the dishonor of the lash. Some, urged by a nice sense of honor, have preferred death to its endurance. I have heard of one man who actually loaded himself with shot and deliberately walked overboard. Among our ship's company the effects of these severe measures showed themselves in frequent desertions, notwithstanding the great risk run by such a bold measure; for, if taken, they were sure to meet with a fearful retribution. Still, many preferred the chance of freedom; some ran off when on shore with the boats, others dropped overboard in the night, and either swam on shore or were drowned. Many others were kept from running away by the strength of their attachment to their old messmates and by the hope of better days. Of those who escaped, some were retaken by the Portuguese, who delighted to hunt them up for a small sum of money. Two of my messmates, named Robert Bell and James Stokes, were taken in this manner. I felt greatly affected at losing their company, for they were pleasant fellows. I felt a peculiar attachment to poor Stokes; he had taught me many things which appertain to seamanship, and had cared for my interests with the faithfulness of a parent. Oh how anxiously did I desire they might not be detected, because I knew, if they were, that they were doomed men. But they were taken by a band of armed Portuguese; barefooted, desponding, broken in spirit, they were brought on board, only to be put in irons immediately. By a fortunate chance they escaped with *fifty* lashes, instead of being flogged through the fleet.

We had another man who escaped, named Richard Suttonwood; he was very profane, and was much in the habit of using the word "bloody;" hence he was nicknamed "Bloody Dick" by his shipmates. Well, Dick ran off. He succeeded in getting on board an English brig in the merchant service. But how chop-fallen was poor Dick when he found that this brig was laden with powder for his own frigate! Resolving to make the best of the matter, he said nothing of his relation to our frigate, but as soon as the brig dropped alongside of the *Macedonian,* he came on board and surrendered himself; by this means he escaped being flogged, as it was usual to pardon a runaway who voluntarily returned to his duty. The crew were all delighted at his return, as he was quite popular among them for his lively disposition and his talents as a comic singer, which last gift is highly prized in a man of war. So joyous were we all at his escape from punishment, that we insisted on his giving a concert, which went off well. Seated on a gun surrounded by scores of the men, he sung a variety of favorite songs, amid the plaudits and *encores* of his rough auditors.

By such means as these, sailors contrive to keep up their spirits amidst constant causes of depression and misery. One is a good singer, another can spin tough forecastle yarns, while a third can crack a joke with sufficient point to call out roars of laughter. But for these interludes, life in a man of war, with severe officers, would be absolutely intolerable; mutiny or desertion would mark the voyages of every such ship. Hence, officers in general highly value your jolly, merry-making, don't-care sort of seamen. They know the effect of their influence in keeping away discontented thought from the minds of a ship's company. One of these official favorites paid our frigate a visit while we lay in Lisbon. We had just finished breakfast, when a number of our men were seen running in high glee towards the main hatchway. Wondering what was going forward, I watched their proceedings with a curious eye. The cause of their joy soon appeared in the person of a short, round-faced, merry-looking tar, who descended the hatchway amid cries of "Hurrah! Here's happy Jack!" As soon as the jovial little man had set his foot on the berth deck, he began a specimen of his vocal powers. The voice of song was as triumphant on board the *Macedonian,* as it was in days of yore in the halls of Ossian. Every voice was hushed, all work was brought to a standstill, while the crew gathered round their favorite, in groups, to listen to his unequalled performances. Happy Jack succeeded, while his visit lasted, in communicating his own joyous feelings to our people, and they parted from him at night with deep regret.

A casual visitor in a man of war, beholding the song, the dance, the revelry of the crew, might judge them to be happy. But I know that these things are often resorted to, because they feel miserable, just to drive away dull care. They do it on the same principle as the slave population in the South, to drown in sensual gratification the voice of misery that groans in the inner man—that lives within, speaking of the indignity offered to its high nature by the chain that eats beyond the flesh—discoursing of the rights of man, of liberty on the free hills of a happier clime: while amidst the gayest negro dance, not a heart among the laughing gang but would beat with high emotions and seize the boon with indescribable avidity, should it be offered its freedom on the spot. So in a man of war, where severe discipline prevails, though cheerfulness smiles at times, it is only the forced merriment of minds ill at ease; minds that would gladly escape the thralldom of the hated service to which they are bound.

Nor is this forced submission to circumstances universal. There are individuals who cannot be reached by these pleasantries; in spite of everything, their spirits will writhe under the gripe of merciless authority. We had a melancholy instance of this species of mind on board our frigate. His name was Hill, the wardroom steward. This man came on board with a resolute purpose to give satisfaction, if possible, to his superiors. He tried his utmost in vain. He was still scolded and cursed, until his condition seemed unendurable. One morning a boy entered the after wardroom, when the first object that met his astonished eye was the body of the steward, all ghastly and bleeding. He had cut his throat, and lay weltering in his gore. The surgeon was called, who pronounced him to be yet alive. The wound was sewed up, the poor sufferer carried to the hospital-ship, which was in attendance on the fleet, where he recovered, to be returned to his former ship, though in another and worse capacity, that of common sailor.

We had on board a colored man whose name was Nugent, who possessed a remarkably fine person, was very intelligent, exceedingly polite in his manners, and easy in his address. He soon grew weary of the caprices of our officers, and ran away. He was taken, however, in rather a curious manner. The officers frequently walked the deck with their spy-glasses. As one of them was spending a few leisure moments in looking at the surrounding shipping, what should appear within the field of his glass, but the person of the fugitive Nugent on the deck of an American vessel! Upon this, a boat was despatched, which soon returned with the crestfallen deserter, who was unceremoniously thrown into irons. By some fortunate chance, however, he escaped a flogging.

Of course, my situation was as unpleasant as that of any other person on board. I could not witness the discomfort and ill-usage of others, without trembling for my own back. I, too, had thoughts of running away, as opportunities frequently offered themselves. But, being ignorant of the Portuguese language, I wisely concluded that my condition among them, if I got clear, would, in respect to my present state, bear about the same analogy as the fire does to the frying-pan. My little adventures on shore gave me full assurance of this fact. I remember going ashore on Good Friday. Like good Catholics, the Portuguese had the masts of their vessels crossed, with effigies of the traitor Judas hanging very significantly at their jib-booms. On shore, they were exhibiting the blasphemous mimicry of the solemn scene of the crucifixion. One was bearing the cross, another a sponge, a third the vinegar. The streets were crowded with images of the saints, to which all reverently bowed. Woe betide that sacrilegious wretch who refused this tribute to their darling images. He *was* sure of being knocked down; he was *not* sure of getting home alive. I was fain to yield my knees to save my skull; so for the time I was as good a Catholic as any of them, at least in the matter of bowing and crossing: it was done, however, with true Protestant mental reservation, and with a sincere determination to prefer my man-of-war's life to a life in Portugal.

On another occasion, some of our officers took me on shore to help them attend to some purchases. After following them a considerable distance, they gave me a small commission to execute, with directions to return to the ship as soon as it was attended to. This was no easy task, however: they had conducted me to a strange part of the city, and I knew scarcely a word of Portuguese. There I stood, then, surrounded only by foreigners, who neither understood my language nor I theirs. All I knew of my destination was, that our boat lay near the Fish-market; so, for Fish-market I inquired. Speaking in English, I asked the first man I met to direct me. He looked at me with the empty stare of an idiot, and passed on. To the next, I said, partly in broken Portuguese and partly in my own tongue, "John," (they call everybody John, whose true name they do not know,) "do show me the fish-market." He could not understand me; so, shrugging his shoulders, he said, "No entender Englis," and passed on. I asked several others, but invariably received a shrug of the shoulder, a shake of the head, and a "no entender Englis," for an answer. I grew desperate, and began to feel as if I had lost myself, when, to my unutterable satisfaction, I saw an English soldier. I ran up to him and said, "Good luck to you; do tell me where the fish-market is, for these stupid Portuguese, bad luck to them, can't understand a word I say; but it is all, no entender Englis." My countryman laughed at seeing my English temper ruffled, and placed me in the way of reaching the fish-market. I hurried thither, when, to my chagrin, the boats were all gone. Here, then, was another difficulty; for, though there were plenty of Portuguese boatmen, they could not understand which ship I wished to reach. Here, however, my fingers did what my tongue refused; our ship had its mainmast out, so, holding up two fingers and pointing to the mast, they at last comprehended me and conveyed me on board. Coming alongside, I gave them what I thought was right; but they and I differed in opinion on that point; they demanded more, with considerable bluster, but the sentry shouted, "Shove off there!" and pointed his musket at them. Whether they thought a reasonable fee, and a timely retreat, better than a contest which might give them the taste of a musket-ball, I cannot determine; at all events, I know that boat never left ship faster than theirs, when they beheld the gleam of the sentry's musket flashing in their dark faces.

Just after this adventure, I came very near being flogged, to my no small alarm. Happening on shore with two more of the officers' servants, named Yates and Skinner, we stayed so late, the ship's boats had all gone off. Finding the boats gone, we strayed back into the city; night came on, and our return until morning was impossible. We had to wander about the city all night, in constant fear of being apprehended by the Portuguese as deserters. To prevent this no very desirable result, my comrades made me a midshipman; for the satisfactory reason, that if an officer was supposed to be in our company, no one would trouble us. The summary process by which I was inducted into my new station, was by means of a stripe carefully marked on my collar with a piece of chalk, to imitate the silver lace on a middy's coat. Thus exalted, I marched my company about Lisbon until dawn, when I again found myself the self-same Samuel Leech, servant to the surgeon of H. M. frigate *Macedonian,* that I was the previous evening, with this additional fact, however, I was now liable to be flogged. So, in the true spirit of a *Jeremy Sneak,* we went on board, where, with due ceremony, we were parted for separate examinations. What tale my fellow-wanderers invented, I know not; for my own part, I told the truth of the matter, excepting that I suppressed that part of it which related to my transformation into an officer. Luckily for us all, one of the party was the first lieutenant's servant; if he flogged one, he must flog the whole. To save the back of his own boy, he let us all escape.

We were now ordered on another cruise. Being in want of men, we resorted to the press-gang which was made up of our most loyal men, armed to the teeth; by their aid we obtained our full numbers. Among them were a few Americans; they were taken without respect to their protections, which were often taken from them and destroyed. Some were released through the influence of the American consul; others, less fortunate, were carried to sea, to their no small chagrin. [1]

The duties of the press-gang completed, we once more weighed anchor, and were soon careering before the gales of the bay of Biscay. Our reception in this proverbially stormy bay was by no means a civil one. We met with an extraordinarily severe gale, in which we came very near foundering. We had just finished dinner, when a tremendous sea broke over us, pouring down the hatchway, sweeping the galley of all its half-cooked contents, then being prepared for the officers' dinner, and covering the berth deck with a perfect flood. It seemed as if old Neptune really intended that wave to sink us to Davy Jones' locker. As the water rolled from

---

[1] To prevent the recovery of these men by their consul, the press-gang usually went ashore on the night previous to our going to sea; so that before they were missed they were beyond his protection. Sometimes they were cleared on our return to port.

side to side within, and the rude waves without beat against her, our good ship trembled from stem to stern, and seemed like a human being gasping for breath in a struggle with death. The women (there were several on board) set up a shriek, a thing they had never done before; some of the men turned pale; others cursed and tried to say witty things; the officers started; orders ran along the ship to man the chain-pumps, and to cut holes through the berth deck to let the water into the hold. These orders being rapidly obeyed, the ship was freed from her danger. The confusion of the moment was followed by laughing and pleasantries. That gale was long spoken of as one of great danger.

It is strange that sailors, who see so much peril, should treat religion with such neglect as it is usual for them to do. When danger is imminent, they send up a cry for help; when it is past, they rarely return a grateful thank-offering. Yet how truly and eloquently has the Psalmist shown, in the 107th Psalm, what should be the moral effect of the wonders of the deep. What but a deep-rooted spiritual perversity prevents such an effect?

The next incident that disturbed the monotony of our sea-life, was of a melancholy character. We had been giving chase to two West Indiamen the whole of one Sabbath afternoon; at night it blew so hard we had to reef top-sails; when a poor fellow, named John Thomson, was knocked from the yard. In falling, he struck some part of the ship, and the wave which opened to receive him, never disclosed his form again. He was a pressed man, an American by birth, greatly beloved by his messmates, by whom his death was as severely felt as when a member of a family dies on shore. His loss created a dull and gloomy atmosphere throughout the ship: it was several days before the hands regained their wonted elasticity of mind and appearance.

My recollections of this cruise are very feeble and indistinct, owing to a severe injury which confined me to my hammock nearly the whole period. The accident which ended in a severe illness had its origin in the following manner. The duty of cleaning knives, plates, dish-covers, etc, for the ward-room, devolved alternately on the boys employed in the ward-room. Having finished this task, one day, in my regular turn, the ward-room steward, a little hot-headed Malay, came to me at dinner-time to inquire for the knives. Not recollecting for the moment, I made no reply; when he angrily pushed me over a sack of bread. In falling my head came in contact with the corner of a locker. Feeling much pain, and the blood flowing freely, I went to Mr. Marsh, the surgeon's mate, who dressed it, and bade me take care of it. Probably it would have healed speedily but for the freak of a sailor a few days after, while holy-stoning the decks. By holy-stoning, I mean cleaning them with stones, which are used for this purpose in men of war. These stones are, some of them, large, with a ring at each end with a rope attached, by which it is pulled backwards and forwards on the wet decks. These large stones are called holy bibles; the smaller hand ones are also called holy-stones, or prayer-books, their shape being something like a book. After the decks are well rubbed with these stones, they are wiped dry with swabs made of rope-yarns. By this means the utmost cleanliness is preserved in the ship. It was customary in our ship, during this scrubbing process, for the boys to wash themselves in a large tub provided for the purpose on the main deck. The men delighted in sousing us with water during this operation. After being wounded, as just mentioned, I endeavored to avoid their briny libations; but one morning, one of the sailors, seeing my anxiety, crept slyly up behind me, and emptied a pail of water directly over my head. That night I began both to look and to feel sick. My messmates said I was sea-sick, and laughed at me. Feeling violent pains in my head, ears and neck, I felt relieved when it was time to turn in. The next morning, being rather behind my usual time in waiting upon the surgeon, he began to scold me. I told him I was unwell. He felt my pulse, examined my tongue, and excused me. Growing worse, my messmates got down my hammock. I entered it very sick; my head and face swelling very large, and my eyes so sunken I could scarcely see.

I remained in this sad situation several weeks, carefully attended by the surgeon, and watched by the men as tenderly as their rough hands could perform the office of nurse. My destiny was considered as being sealed, both by the crew and by myself. I was much troubled at the thought of dying: it seemed dark and dreary to enter the valley of the shadow of death without the presence of a Saviour. To relieve my feelings, I frequently repeated the Lord's prayer, taught me by my indulgent mother in my earlier and brighter years. But my mind was dark and disconsolate; there were none among that kind-hearted but profligate crew to point my soul to its proper rest.

While lying in this state, my life hanging in a doubtful balance, one of the crew, named Black Tom, an African, was taken sick. His hammock was hung up in the sick bay, a part of the main deck appropriated to hospital purposes. Poor Tom, having a constitution already undermined by former excesses, soon fell under the attack of disease. He was then sewed up in his hammock, with some shot at his feet: at sundown the ship's bell pealed a melancholy note, the ship was "hove to," all hands mustered on deck, but myself; and, amid the most profound silence, the body of the departed sailor was laid upon the grating and launched into the great deep, the resting-place of many a bold head. A plunge, a sudden opening in the water, followed by an equally sudden return of the disparted waves, and Black Tom was gone forever from his shipmates! In a few moments the yards were braced round, and our frigate was cutting her way again through the wide ocean waste. It seemed to me that she was soon destined to heave to again, that I might also be consigned to an ocean grave. But in this I was happily disappointed. By the blessing of a watchful Providence, the aid of a sound constitution, assisted by the skill of our surgeon and the kindness of my shipmates, I was at last able to leave my hammock. Shortly after our return to Lisbon, I was pronounced fit for duty, and the surgeon having obtained another boy, I was placed on the quarter deck, in the capacity of messenger, or errand boy for the captain and his officers.

With my return to active life, came my exposure to hardships, and, what I dreaded still more, to punishment. Some of the boys were to be punished on the main deck; the rest were ordered forward to witness it, as usual. Being so far aft that I could not hear the summons, as a matter of course, I remained at my post. The hawk-eye of the lieutenant missed me, and in a rage he ordered me to be sent for to receive a flogging for my absence. Excuse was vain; for, such was the fiendish temper of this brutal officer, he only wanted the shadow of a reason for dragging the poor helpless boys of his charge to the grating. While I stood in trembling expectation of being degraded by the hated cat, a summons from the captain providentially called off our *brave* boy-flogger, and I escaped. The offense was never mentioned afterwards. The reader can easily perceive how such a constant exposure to the lash must embitter a seaman's life.

Already, since the *Macedonian* had been in commission, had she changed captains twice. Why it so happened, it is not in my power to explain; but while at Lisbon, after the cruise last mentioned, our present captain was superseded by Captain John S. Car-den. His arrival excited a transitory hope of a brighter lot, as he was an older man than the others, and, as we vainly trusted, a kinder one. Here, however, we were mistaken; he was like all the rest, the same heartless, unfeeling lover of whip discipline. At first the men under sentence tried their powers at flattery with the grave old man; but he was too experienced a sea-dog to be cajoled

SAMUEL LEECH

by a long-faced sailor under sentence: when, therefore, they told him he was a kind-hearted *fatherly* gentleman, he only replied by a most provoking laugh, and by saying they were a set of very undutiful sons.

Captain Carden was mercilessly severe in punishing theft. He would on no account forgive any man for this crime, but would flog the thief almost to death. Of this, we soon had a cruel instance. A midshipman named Gale, a most rascally, unprincipled fellow, found his pocket handkerchief in possession of one of the crew. He charged the man with stealing it. It was in vain that the poor wretch asserted that he found it under his hammock. He was reported as a thief; a court-martial sat upon him, and returned the shamefully disproportionate sentence of three hundred lashes through the fleet, and one year's imprisonment! Any of my shipmates who are living, will certify to the truth of this statement, brutal and improbable as it may appear.

Nor was that sentence a dead letter; the unhappy man endured it to the letter. Fifty were laid on alongside of the *Macedonian,* in conformity with a common practice of inflicting the most strokes at the first ship, in order that the gory back of the criminal may strike the more terror into the crews of the other ships. This poor tortured man bore two hundred and twenty, and was pronounced by the attending surgeon unfit to receive the rest. Galled, bruised, and agonized as he was, he besought him to suffer the infliction of the remaining eighty, that he might not be called to pass through the degrading scene again; but this prayer was denied! He was brought on board, and when his wounds were healed, the captain, Shylock-like, determined to have the whole pound of flesh, ordered him to receive the remainder.

But for my desire to present the reader with a true exhibition of life on board a British man of war, it would be my choice to suppress these disgusting details of cruelty and punishment. But this is impossible; I must either draw a false picture or describe them. I choose the latter, in the hope that giving publicity to these facts will exert a favorable influence on the already improving discipline of ships of war.

The case of our ship's drummer will illustrate the hopelessness of our situation under such officers as commanded our ship; it will show that implicit, uncomplaining submission was our only resource. This drummer, being seized up for some petty offense, demanded, what no captain can refuse, to be tried by a court-martial; in the hope, probably, of escaping altogether. The officers laughed among each other, and when, a few days afterwards, the poor, affrighted man offered to withdraw the demand and take six dozen lashes, they coolly remarked, "The drummer is sick of his bargain."

He would have been a wiser man had he never made it; for the court-martial sentenced him to receive two hundred lashes through the fleet—a punishment ostensibly for his first offense, but really for his insolence (?) in demanding a trial by court-martial. Such was the administration of justice (?) on board the *Macedonian*.

"Why did not your crew rise in resistance to such cruelty?" is a question which has often been proposed to me, when relating these facts to my American friends. To talk of mutiny on shore is an easy matter; but to excite it on shipboard is to rush on to certain death. Let it be known that a man has dared to breathe the idea, and he is sure to swing at the yard-arm. Some of our men once saw six mutineers hanging at the yard-arm at once, in a ship whose crew exhibited the incipient beginnings of mutiny. Let mutiny be successful, the government will employ its whole force, if needful, in hunting down the mutineers; their blood, to the last drop, is the terrible retribution it demands for this offense. That demand is sure to be met, as was the case with the crew of the *Hermione*[1] frigate, and with the crew of the ill-fated *Bounty,* whose history is imprinted on the memory of the whole civilized world. With such tragedies flitting before our eyes, who need ask why we did not resist?

Just before we left Lisbon for another cruise, my position was once more changed by my appointment to the post of servant to the sailing-master; whose boy, for some offense or other, was flogged and turned away. Here, too, the captain procured a fine band, composed of Frenchmen, Italians and Germans, taken by the Portuguese from a French vessel. These musicians consented to serve, on condition of being excused from fighting, and on a pledge of exemption from being flogged. They used to play to the captain during his dinner hour; the party to be amused usually consisting of the captain and one or two invited guests from the wardroom; except on Sundays, when he chose to honor the ward-

---

[1] The crew of this vessel mutinied, killed their officers, and run the ship into a Spanish port, where she fell into the hands of the Spaniards, then at war with England. Large rewards were offered for these mutineers; many were taken, and all who were taken suffered the penalty of death (1797).

room with his august presence. The band then played for the
wardroom. They also played on deck whenever we entered or left a
port. On the whole, their presence was an advantage to the crew,
since their spirit-stirring strains served to spread an occasional
cheerful influence over them. Soon after they came on board, we
had orders to proceed to sea again on another cruise.

CHAPTER FOUR

A FEW days after we had fairly got out to sea, the thrilling cry of "A man overboard!" ran through the ship with electrical effect; it was followed by another cry of, "Heave out a rope!" then by still another, of "Cut away the life buoy!" Then came the order, "Lower a boat!" Notwithstanding the rapidity of these commands, and the confusion occasioned by the anticipated loss of a man, they were rapidly obeyed. The ship was then hove to. But that time, however, the cause of all this excitement was at a considerable distance from the ship. It was a poor Swede, named Logholm, who, while engaged in lashing the larboard anchor stock, lost his hold and fell into the sea. He could not swim; but, somehow, he managed to keep afloat until the boat reached him, when he began to sink. The man at the bow ran his boat hook down, and caught the drowning man by his clothes: his clothes tearing, the man lost his hold, and the Swede once more sunk. Again the active bowsman ran the hook down, leaning far over the side; fortunately, he got hold of his shirt collar: dripping, and apparently lifeless, they drew him into the boat. He was soon under the surgeon's care, whose skill restored him to animation and to life. It was a narrow escape!

Rising one morning, I heard the men talking about having been called to quarters during the night. They said a strange vessel having appeared, the drums beat to quarters, the guns were got ready, those great lanterns, which are placed on the main deck, called battle lanterns, were got out, and the officers began to muster the men at each division; when they discovered the supposed vessel of war to be nothing more than a large merchant ship. Upon this the hands were sent below. All this was news to me; I had slept through all the noise, confusion and bustle of the night, utterly ignorant of the whole matter. It was fortunate for me that the real character of the strange ship was discovered before my name was called, otherwise the morning would have found me at the gratings under punishment. Never was boy happier than myself, when made acquainted with my hair-breadth escape from the lash.

We had now reached the island of Madeira, occupied by the Portuguese, and producing fine oranges, grapes and wine. It is some sixty miles in length, about forty in breadth; the climate is hot, but salubrious; its harbor, or rather roadstead, is by no means commodious or safe—so that our stay was short. Here, the Portuguese lad who had supplied my place as servant to the surgeon, was sent on shore, for attempting a crime unfit to be mentioned in these pages, but quite common among the Spaniards and Portuguese. My old master made an effort to obtain me again, but did not succeed,

Sailing from Madeira, we next made St. Michael's. At this pace we had an increase to our crew, in the person of a fine, plump boy—born to the wife of one of our men. The captain christened the new comer, Michael, naming him after the island. This birth was followed by another. Whether the captain did not like the idea of such interesting episodes in sea life, or whether any other motive inspired him, I cannot tell; but when, shortly after, we returned to Lisbon, he ordered all the women home to England, by a ship just returning thither. Before this, however, one of our little Tritons had died, and found a grave under the billows, leaving its disconsolate mother in a state little short of distraction, A man of war is no place for a woman.

Short cruises are very popular with man-of-war's men. On many accounts they love being in harbor; on others they prefer being at sea. In harbor they have to work all day, but in return for this they have the whole night for sleep. At sea, the whole time is divided into five watches of four hours each, and two shorter ones, called dog watches, of two hours each, or from four to six and from six to eight, P.M. The design of these dog watches is to alternate the time, so that each watch may have a fair proportion of every night below.

While at our station this time, our old friend, Bob Hammond, met with some little difficulty, which we will here make matter of record. He was below, and one of his messmates did something that vexed him exceedingly. Now Bob was not a man to bear vexa-tions tamely, where he had the power to resist them; so, lifting his huge fist, he struck at the offender; missing his real opponent, the blow fell upon another who stood near him. Bob was too much of a bully to offer any apology; he merely laughed, and remarked that he had "killed two birds with one stone."

Whether the bird, who, in Bob's figurative language, was killed, did not like being called a bird, or whether he conceived a strong dislike to being a mark for Bob to shoot at, is not for me to say; but he certainly disliked the one or the other, for the next morning he reported the matter to the officers, which complaint was considered a most unsailor-like act by the whole crew.

Fighting was a punishable offense, so Bob was called up the next morning. The captain mentioned what was reported concern-ing him. He acknowledged it was all true, and without any signs of contrition said, "I only killed two birds with one stone." The angry captain ordered two dozen lashes to be laid on; it was done with-out extorting a sigh or a groan. He was then loosed from the grat-ing, and questioned; but he merely replied, in a gruff tone, that "the man who reported him was a blackguard!" For this, he was seized up again and another dozen lashes inflicted; he bore them with the same dogged and imperturbable air. Finding it impossible to extort any acknowledgment from the stubborn tar, the captain ordered him below.

About the same time one of our crew, named Jack Sadler, a fine, noble-hearted seaman, growing weary of the service, deter-mined to desert. Dropping into the water, he began swimming to-wards the shore. It was not very dark, and he was discovered; the sentry was ordered to fire at him, which he did, but missed his prey. A boat was next lowered, which soon overtook and dragged him on board. The officer commanding the boat said, "Well, Mr. Sadler, you thought you had got away, did you?"

"You are not so sure that you have me now," replied Sadler, as he sprung over the side of the boat. Nor would they have captured him, had not another ship's boat arrived to their assistance.

The next day, he was seized up and received three dozen lashes, which, considering his offense, was a very light punish-ment. I suppose that his noble bearing, his lion-hearted courage, and his undaunted manner, produced a favorable feeling in the captain's mind; especially as he afterwards became his favorite—a fancy man —as those men are called who win the favor of their su-perior officer.

One of Sadler's failings was that too prevalent evil among seamen, drunkenness. Soon after the above affair, he got drunk. Being seen by the captain, he was ordered to be put in irons. Sadler
was Bob Hammond's messmate; this worthy, finding his comrade
in trouble, made himself drunk, and purposely placed himself in
the way of the officers, that he might be put in irons also, to keep
his friend Sadler company. The plan succeeded. Bob had his wish,
and the two fearless tars were soon ironed together. Nothing
daunted, they began to sing, and through the whole night they
kept up such a hallooing, shouting and singing as might have
served for a whole company of idle roisterers. Being near the
ward-room, they prevented the officers from sleeping nearly all
night.

As usual, after being in irons, they were brought up for punishment the next morning. "Well, Mr. Sadler," said the captain,
"you were drunk, were you, last night? "

"I was, sir," replied the offender.

Had he been any other man, he would have been ordered to
strip: as it was, the captain proceeded:

"Do you feel sorry for it, sir?"

"I do, sir."

"Will you try to keep sober if I forgive you?" continued Captain
Carden.

"I will try, sir."

"Then, sir, I forgive you." And no doubt he was glad to witness
that contrition in his favorite which made it consistent to forgive
him. Having dismissed Sadler, he turned to Hammond: assuming
a sterner look and a harsher voice, he said, in a tone of irony,
"Well, Mr. Hammond, you got drunk last night, did you, sir?"

Bob shrugged up his shoulders, and removed his enormous
quid into a convenient position for speaking, and then replied, "I
can't say but that I had a horn of malt."

The captain looked thunder at the stalwart man, as he answered, A horn of malt, you rascal! What do you call a horn of
malt?"

"When I was in Bengal, Madras, and Batavia," said he, "I used
to get some stuff called arrack—we used to call it a horn of malt;
but this was some good rum."

Bob's manner was so exquisitely ridiculous while delivering
this harangue, that both officers and men broke out into an invol-

untary laugh. The captain looked confounded, but recovering himself, he said to Mr. Hope, the first lieutenant, "Put that rascal in irons; it is of no use to flog him."

One of the peculiarities of Captain Carden was an ardent desire to have a crew of picked, first-rate men. The shiftless, slovenly-seaman was his abhorrence. Had he dared, he would gladly have given all such their discharge; as it was, he never attempted their recovery, by offering a reward for their detection, if they ran away; while he spared no pains to catch an able, active, valuable man like Sadler. He even gave these drones opportunity to escape, by sending them on shore at Lisbon, to cut stuff to make brooms for sweeping the deck. The men sent out on these expeditions were nicknamed "broomers." Now, although Bob Hammond was as expert a sailor as any man in the ship, yet his unconquerable audacity made the captain fear his influence, and wish to get rid of him; hence, a few days after this drunken spree, Bob was called on deck to go with the broomers. "You may go, Mr. Hammond," said the captain, eyeing him in a very expressive manner," with these fellows to cut broom."

Bob understood the hint perfectly, and replied, "Aye, aye, sir, and I will cut a long handle to it." I scarcely need remark that the broomers returned without Bob. Whether he remained on shore to cut the long handle, or for some other purpose, he never informed us: certain it is, however, that the presence of Bob Hammond never darkened the decks of the *Macedonian* again.

About this time the prevailing topic of conversation among our men and officers was the probability of a war with America. The prevailing feeling through the whole fleet was that of confidence in our own success, and of contempt for the inferior naval force of our anticipated enemies. Every man, and especially the officers, predicted, as his eye glanced proudly on the fine fleet which was anchored off Lisbon, a speedy and successful issue to the approaching conflict.

We now received orders to sail to Norfolk, Virginia, with dispatches. The, voyage was accomplished without any occurrence of note. We found ourselves on the American coast, with no very pleasant impressions. It was late in the fall, and the transition from the mild, soft climate of Spain and Portugal, to the bleak, sharp atmosphere of the coast of Virginia, was anything but delightful.

The most disagreeable duty in the ship was that of holystoning the decks on cold, frosty mornings. Our movements were never more elastic than when at this really severe task. As usual, it gave occasion to a variety of forecastle yarns about cold stations. Among these was one which was attested by many witnesses, and there can be no doubt of its truth.

A British frigate was once stationed in a cold climate. The first lieutenant was a complete tyrant, delighting in everything that caused the crew to suffer. Among other things, he took especial care to make the work of holy-stoning as painful as possible, by forcing them to continue at it much longer than was necessary. Although he had no watch on deck, he would contrive to be up in season to annoy the men with his hated presence. One morning, the weather being unusually severe, the men sprang to their task with unwonted agility, and contrived to finish it before the appearance of their persecutor. To their vexation, however, just as they had completed their work, he bounced on deck, with a peremptory order to wash the decks all over a second time.

The men dropped on their knees with the holy-stones, and prayed, as the tyrant went below, that he might never come on deck again alive. Whether God heard the cry of the oppressed crew, or whether it was the action of the ordinary natural laws, the reader must determine for himself; but when the lieutenant again appeared on deck, he was brought up "feet foremost," to be buried. He was taken sick that morning: his disease baffled the skill of the surgeon, and in a few days he was a corpse. The opinion that he died a monument of the divine displeasure against cruel, hard-hearted men of power, and of disregard for the miseries and tears of the oppressed poor, is at least worthy of serious consideration.

Soon after we had descried land, an American pilot came on board to pilot us into Hampton Roads. The sound of our own familiar tongue from a stranger, was very agreeable to men who had been accustomed to hear the semi-barbarous lingo of the Portuguese, and a thrill of home remembrances shot through our hearts, as, stepping on deck, the pilot exclaimed, "It is very cold! "

While at anchor in Hampton Roads, we fared well. Boats were alongside every day with plenty of beef and pork, which was declared, by universal consent, to be infinitely superior to what we obtained from Portugal. Our men said that the Yankee pork would swell in the pot, which they very sagely accounted for on the supposition that the pigs were killed at the full of the moon. But I suppose that Virginia corn had more to do in this matter than lunar influences; though our men most doggedly maintained the contrary and more mystical opinion.

The principal draw-back on the enjoyment of our stay at Norfolk, was the denial of liberty to go on shore. The strictest care was taken to prevent all communication with the shore, either personally or by letter. The reason of this prohibition was a fear lest we should desert. Many of our crew were Americans: some of these were pressed men; others were much dissatisfied with the severity, not to say cruelty, of our discipline; so that a multitude of the crew were ready to give "leg bail," as they termed it, could they have planted their feet on American soil. Hence our liberty was restrained.

Our officers never enjoyed better cheer than during our stay at this port. Besides feasting among themselves on the fine fat beef, geese and turkeys, which came alongside in abundance, they exchanged visits with Commodore Decatur and his officers, of the frigate *United States,* then lying at Norfolk. These visits were seasons of much wassail and feasting. I remember overhearing Commodore Decatur and the captain of the *Macedonian* joking about taking each other's ship, in case of a war; and some of the crew said that a bet of a beaver hat passed between them on the issue of such a conflict. They probably little thought that this joking over a wine-cup, would afterwards be cracked in earnest, in a scene of blood and carnage.

It was at this port that the difficulty between the British ship *Leopard* and the American frigate *Chesapeake* took place. Several American seamen, having escaped from the former, took refuge on board the latter. The captain of the *Leopard* demanded their restoration; the captain of the *Chesapeake* refused submission to the demand. The *Leopard* fired into the frigate, which, being of inferior force, struck to her opponent. As it was a time of peace, the *Chesapeake* was not kept as a prize; the claimed men were taken from her, and she was restored. This was among the circumstances which led to the war of 1812.

The dispatches delivered, and the object of the voyage accomplished, we once more put to sea; having first laid in a liberal store of our favorite beef, together with a quantity of Virginia beans, called Calavances, which were in high favor with our men. To those of our crew who were Americans, this was rather an unpleasant event. Like the fabled Tantalus, they had the cup at their mouths, but it receded before they could taste its contents. They had been at the threshold of "home, sweet home," but had not been permitted to step within its doors. Some of them felt this very keenly, especially a boy, who belonged to New York, named Jesse Lloyd. In truth, it was a hard lot.

A quick winter passage brought us to Lisbon, where the arrival of the English mail-bag, and orders to proceed to England with a convoy of merchantmen, put us all into a tolerably good humor.

The arrival of the mail-bag is a season of peculiar interest on board a man of war. It calls the finer feelings of human nature into exercise. It awakens conjugal, fraternal, and filial affection in almost every breast. The men crowd around, as the letters are distributed, and he was pronounced a happy fellow whose name was read off by the distributor; while those who had none, to hide their disappointment, would jocularly offer to buy those belonging to their more fortunate messmates.

During the two years of our absence I had received several letters from my mother, which afforded me much satisfaction. To these I had faithfully replied. I now experienced the advantage of the primary education I had received when a boy. Many of my shipmates could neither read nor write, and were, in consequence either altogether deprived of the privilege of intercourse with their friends, or were dependent on the kindness of others, to read and write for them. For these I acted as a sort of scribe. I also solaced many weary hours by reading such works as could be obtained from the officers; and sometimes I perused the Bible and prayer book which my mother so wisely placed in my chest, on the eve of my departure. The pack of cards, which so inappropriately accompanied them, I had loaned to one of the officers, who took the liberty to keep them. This was, perhaps, more fortunate than otherwise, since their possession might have led to their use, and their use might have excited a propensity to gambling, which would have ended in my ruin.

After remaining a very short time at Lisbon, we one morning fired a gun to give notice to our convoy to get under weigh. Immediately the harbor was alive with noise and activity. The song of the sailors weighing anchor, the creaking of pulleys, the flapping of the sails, the loud, gruff voices of the officers, and the splashing of the waters, created what was to us, now that we were "homeward bound," a sweet harmony of sounds. Amid all this animation, our own stately frigate spread her bellying sails to a light but favoring breeze; with colors flying, our band playing lively airs, and the captain with his speaking trumpet urging the lagging merchant-ships to more activity, we passed gaily through the large fleet consigned to our care. In this gallant style we scudded past the straggling ruins of old Lisbon, which still bore marks of the earthquake that destroyed it. Very soon the merry fishermen, who abound in the Tagus, were far at our stern. Next, we glided past the tall granite pinnacles of towering mount Cintra; the high-lands passed from our vision like the scenes in a panorama, and in a few hours, instead of the companionship of the large flocks of gulls, which abound in this river, we were attended by only here and there one of these restless wanderers of the deep. We were fairly at sea, and, what was the more inspiring, we were enjoying the luxury of fond anticipation. Visions of many an old fire-side, of many a humble hearth-stone, poor, but precious, flitted across the visions of our crew that night. Hardships, severe discipline, were for the time forgotten in the dreams of hope. Would that I could say that everything in every mind was thus absorbed in pleasure! There were minds that writhed under what is never forgotten. Like the scar, that time may heal, but not remove, the flogged man forgets not that he has been degraded; the whip, when it scarred the flesh, went farther; it wounded the spirit; it struck the *man;* it begat a sense of degradation he must carry with him to his grave. We had many such on board our frigate; their laugh sounded empty, and sometimes their look became suddenly vacant in the midst of hilarity. It was the whip entering the soul anew. But the most of our crew were, for the time, happy. They were homeward bound!

CHAPTER FIVE

AFTER running a few days before a fair wind, the delightful cry of "Land ho!" was heard from the mast-head; a cry always pleasant to the inhabitant of a ship, but most especially so when the distant hills are those of his native land. Soon after the cry of the man aloft, the land became dimly visible from the deck, and our eyes glistened, as the bright, emerald fields of old England, in all the glory of their summer beauty, lay spread out before us. Ascending the British Channel, we soon made the spacious harbor of Plymouth, where we came to an anchor. One of our convoy, however, by some unskilful management, ran ashore at the mouth of the harbor, where she went to pieces.

We found Plymouth to be a naval station of considerable importance, well fortified, possessing extensive barracks for the accommodation of the military, and having a magnificent dock-yard, abundantly supplied with the means of building and refitting the wooden walls.

Nothing would have afforded me a higher gratification, than a trip to the pleasant fields and quiet hearth-sides of dear old Bladen. I longed to pour out my pent-up griefs into the bosom of my mother, and to find that sympathy which is sought in vain in the cold, unfeeling world. This privilege was, however, denied to all. No one could obtain either leave of absence or money, since a man of war is never "paid off" until just before she proceeds to sea. But, feeling heartily tired of the service, I wrote to my mother, requesting her to endeavor to procure my discharge. This, with the promptitude of maternal affection, she pledged herself to do at the earliest possible opportunity. How undying is a mother's love!

When a man of war is in port, it is usual to grant the crew occasional liberty to go on shore. These indulgences are almost invariably abused for purposes of riot, drunkenness and debauchery; rarely does it happen, but that these shore sprees end in bringing "poor Jack" into difficulty of some sort; for, once on shore, he is like an uncaged bird, as gay and quite as thoughtless. He will then follow out the dictates of passions and appetites, let them lead him whither they may. Still, there are exceptions; there are a few who spend their time more rationally. Were the principles of modern temperance fully triumphant among sailors, they would all do so.

I resolved not to abuse my liberty as I saw others doing; so when, one fine Sabbath morning, I had obtained leave from our surly first lieutenant, I chose the company of a brother to a messmate, named Rowe, who lived at Plymouth. At the request of my messmate, I called to see him. He received me very kindly, and took me in company with his children into the fields, where the merry notes of the numerous birds, the rich perfume of the blooming trees, the tall, green hedges, and the modest primroses, cowslips and violets, which adorned the banks on the road-side, filled me with inexpressible delight. True, this was not the proper manner of spending a Sabbath day, but it was better than it would have been to follow the example of my shipmates generally, who were carousing in the tap-rooms of the public houses.

At sunset I went on board and walked aft to the lieutenant, to report myself. He appeared surprised to see me on board so early and so perfectly sober, and jocosely asked me why I did not get drunk and be like a sailor. Merely smiling, I retired to my berth, thinking it was very queer for an officer to laugh at a boy for doing right, and feeling happy within myself because I had escaped temptation.

By and by, three other boys, who had been ashore, returned, in a state which a sailor would call "three sheets in the wind." They blustered, boasted of the high time they had enjoyed, and roundly laughed at me for being so unlike a man-of-war's-man; while they felt as big as any man on board. The next morning, however, they looked rather chop-fallen, when the captain, who had accidentally seen their drunken follies on shore, ordered them to be flogged, and forbade their masters to send them ashore while we remained at Plymouth. Now, then, it was pretty evident who had the best cruise; the joke was on the other side; for while their drunken behavior cost them a terrible whipping and a loss of liberty, my temperance gained me the *real* approbation of my officers, and more liberty than ever, since after that day I had to go on shore to do errands for their masters, as well as for my own. The young sailor may learn from this fact the benefit of temperance, and the folly of getting drunk, for the sake of being called a fine fellow.

My frequent visits to the shore gave me many opportunities to run away; while my dislike of everything about the *Macedonian* inspired me with the disposition to improve them. Against this measure my judgment wisely remonstrated, and, happily for my well being, succeeded. Such an attempt would inevitably have been followed by my recovery, since a handsome bounty was paid for the delivery of every runaway. There are always a sufficient number to be found who will engage in pursuit for the sake of money—such men as the Canadian landlord, described by Rev. Wm, Lighton, in his interesting narrative,[1] a work with which, no doubt, most of *my* readers are acquainted, since it has enjoyed an immense circulation. Endurance, therefore, was the only rational purpose I could form.

Perhaps the hope of a speedy discharge, through my mother's efforts, tended somewhat to this result in my case; besides, my situation had become somewhat more tolerable from the fact, that by dint of perseverance in a civil and respectful behavior, I had gained the good will both of the officers and crew. Yet, with this advantage, it was a miserable situation.

There are few worse places than a man of war, for the favorable development of the moral character in a boy. Profanity, in its most revolting aspect; licentiousness, in its most shameful and beastly garb; vice, in the worst of its Proteus-like shapes, abound there. While scarcely a moral restraint is thrown round the victim, the meshes of temptation are spread about his path in every direction. Bad as things are at sea, they are worse in port. There, boatloads of denied and defiling women are permitted to come alongside; the men, looking over the side, select whoever best pleases his lustful fancy, and by paying her fare, he is allowed to take and keep her on board as his paramour, until the ship is once more ordered to sea. Many of these lost, unfortunate creatures are in the

---

[1] Narrative of the Life and Sufferings of William B. Lighton (an Englishman), a private in the 60th Regiment—the Rifles.—Troy, N. Y., 1846. He enlisted at 16, in 1820.

springtime of life, some of them are not without pretensions to beauty. The ports of Plymouth and Portsmouth are crowded with these fallen beings. How can a boy be expected to escape pollution, surrounded by such works of darkness? Yet, some parents send their children to sea because they are ungovernable ashore! Better send them to the house of correction.

There is one aspect in which life at sea and life in port materially differ. At sea, a sense of danger, an idea of insecurity, is ever present to the mind; in harbor, a sense of security lulls the sailor into indulgence. He feels perfectly safe. Yet, even in harbor, danger sometimes visits the fated ship, stealing upon her like the spirit of evil. This remark was fearfully illustrated in the loss of the *Royal George,* which sunk at Spithead, near Portsmouth, on the 29th of August, 1782.

This splendid line of battle ship of one hundred and eight guns, had arrived at Spithead. Needing some repairs, she was *"heeled down"* or inclined on one side, to allow the workmen to work on her sides. Finding more needed to be done to the copper sheathing than was expected, the sailors were induced to heel her too much. While in this state, she was struck by a slight squall; the cannon rolled over to the depressed side; her ports were open, she filled with water, and sunk to the bottom!

This dreadful catastrophe occurred about ten o'clock in the morning. The brave Admiral Kempenfeldt was writing in his cabin; most of the crew, together with some three hundred women, were between decks: these nearly all perished. Captain Waghorn, her commander, was saved; his son, one of her lieutenants, was lost. Those who were on the upper deck were picked up by the boats of the fleet, but nearly one thousand souls met with a sudden and untimely end. The poet Cowper has celebrated this melancholy event in the following beautiful lines:

> Toll for the brave!
>> The brave that are no more!
> All sunk beneath the wave,
>> Fast by their native shore.
>
> Eight hundred of the brave,
>> Whose courage well was tried,
> Had made the vessel heel,
>> And laid her on her side.
>
> A land breeze shook the shrouds,
>> And she was overset;

Down went the *Royal George*,
    With all her crew complete.

Toll for the brave—
    Brave Kempenfeldt is gone,
His last sea fight is fought—
    His work of glory done.

It was not in the battle;
    No tempest gave the shock;
She sprang no fatal leak;
    She ran upon no rock.

His sword was in its sheath;
    His fingers held the pen,
When Kempenfeldt went down,
    With twice four hundred men.

Weigh the vessel up,
    Once dreaded by our foes!
And mingle with our cup
    The tear that England owes.

Her timbers yet are sound,
    And she may float again,
Full charged with England's thunder,
    And plough the distant main.

But Kempenfeldt is gone,
    His victories are o'er;
And he, and his eight hundred,
    Shall plough the wave no more.

To return to my narrative: Our ship, having been at sea two years, needed overhauling. She was therefore taken into one of the splendid dry docks in the Plymouth dock-yard, while the crew were placed, for the time being, on board an old hulk. A week or two sufficed for this task, when we returned to our old quarters. She looked like a new ship, having been gaily painted within and without. We, too, soon got newly rigged; for orders had reached us from the Admiralty office to prepare for sea, and we were paid off. Most of the men laid out part of their money in getting new clothing; some of it went to buy pictures, looking-glasses, crockery ware, etc, to ornament our berths, so that they bore some resemblance to a cabin. The women were ordered ashore, and we were once more ready for sea.

The practice of paying seamen at long intervals, is the source of many evils. Among these, is the opportunity given to pursers to practice extortion on the men—an opportunity they are not slow in improving. The spendthrift habits of most sailors leave them with a barely sufficient quantity of clothing, for present purposes, when they ship. If the cruise is long, they are, consequently, obliged to draw from the purser. This gentleman is ever ready to supply them, but at ruinous prices. Poor articles with high prices are to be found in his hands; these poor Jack must take of necessity, because he cannot get his wages until he is paid off. Hence, what with poor articles, high charges and *false* charges, the purser almost always has a claim which makes Jack's actual receipts for two or three years' service, woefully small. Were he paid at stated periods, he could make his own purchases as he needed them. The sailor is aware of this evil, but he only shows his apprehension of it in his usually good-humored manner. If he sees a poor, ill-cut garment, he will laugh, and say it "looks like a purser's shirt on a handspike." These are small matters, but they go to make up the sum total of a seaman's life, and should therefore be remedied as far as possible.

Our preparations all completed, the hoarse voice of the boatswain rang through the ship, crying, "All hands up anchor, ahoy!" In a trice, the capstan bars were shipped, the fifer was at his station playing a lively tune, the boys were on the main deck holding on to the "nippers," ready to pass them to the men, who put them round the "messenger" and cable; then, amid the cries of "Walk round! Heave away, my lads!" accompanied by the shrill music of the fife, the anchor rose from its bed, and was soon dangling under our bows. The sails were then shaken out, the ship brought before the wind, and we were once more on our way to sea. We were directed to cruise off the coast of France this time; where, as we were then at war with the French, we were likely to find active service.

We first made the French port of Rochelle; from thence, we sailed to Brest, which was closely blockaded by a large British fleet, consisting of one three-decker, with several seventy-fours, besides frigates and small craft. We joined this fleet, and came to an anchor in Basque Roads, to assist in the blockade. Our first object was to bring a large French fleet, greatly superior to us in size and numbers, to an engagement. With all our maneuvering, we could not succeed in enticing them from their snug berth in the harbor of Brest, where they were safely moored, defended by a heavy fort, and by a chain crossing the harbor, to prevent the ingress of any force that might be bold enough to attempt to cut them out. Sometimes we sent a frigate or two as near their fort as they dared to venture, in order to entice them out; at other times, the whole fleet would get under weigh and stand out to sea; but without success. The Frenchmen were either afraid we had a larger armament than was visible to them, or they had not forgotten the splendid victories of Nelson at the Nile and Trafalgar. Whatever they thought, they kept their ships beyond the reach of our guns. Sometimes, however, their frigates would creep outside the forts, when we gave them chase, but seldom went beyond the exchange of a few harmless shots. This was what our men called "boy's play;" and they were heartily glad when we were ordered to return to Plymouth.

After just looking into Plymouth harbor, our orders were countermanded, and we returned to the coast of France. Having accomplished about one half the distance, the man at the mast-head cried out, "Sail ho!"

"Where away?" (What direction?) responded the officer of the deck. The man having replied, the officer again asked, "What does she look like? "

"She looks small; I cannot tell, sir."

In a few minutes the officer hailed again, by shouting, "Mast-head, there! what does she look like? "

"She looks like a small sail-boat, sir."

This was rather a novel announcement; for what could a small sail-boat do out on the wide ocean? But a few minutes convinced us that it was even so; for, from the deck, we could see a small boat, with only a man and a boy on board. They proved to be two French prisoners of war, who had escaped from an English prison, and, having stolen a small boat, were endeavoring to make this perilous voyage to their native home. Poor fellows! They looked sadly disappointed at finding themselves once more in British hands. They had already been in prison for some time; they were now doomed to go with us, in sight of their own sunny France, and then be torn away again, carried to England, and imprisoned until the close of the war. No wonder they looked sorrowful, when, after having hazarded life for home and liberty, they found both snatched from them in a moment, by their unlucky rencontre with our frigate. I am sure we should all have been glad to have missed them. But this is only one of the consequences of war.

Having joined the blockading fleet again, we led the same sort of life as before: now at anchor, then giving chase; now standing in shore, and anon standing out to sea; firing, and being fired at, without once coming into action.

Determined to accomplish some exploit or other, our captain ordered an attempt to be made at cutting out some of the French small craft that lay in shore. We were accustomed to send out our barges almost every night, in search of whatever prey they might capture. But on this occasion the preparations were more formidable than usual. The oars were muffled; the boat's crew increased, and every man was armed to the teeth. The cots were got ready on board, in case any of the adventurers should return wounded. Cots are used to sleep in by ward-room officers and captains; midshipmen and sailors using hammocks. But a number of cots are always kept in a vessel of war, for the benefit of wounded men; they differ from a hammock, in being square at the bottom, and consequently more easy. The service on which the barge was sent being extremely dangerous, the cots were got ready to receive the wounded, should there be any; but notwithstanding these expressive preparations, the brave fellows went off in as fine spirits as if they had been going on shore for a drunken spree. Such is the contempt of danger that prevails among sailors.

We had no tidings of this adventure until morning, when I was startled by hearing three cheers from the watch on deck; these were answered by three more from a party that seemed approaching us. I ran on deck just as our men came alongside with their bloodless prize—a lugger, laden with French brandy, wine and Castile soap. They had made this capture without difficulty; for the crew of the lugger made their escape in a boat, on the first intimation of danger. As this was our first prize, we christened her the *Young Macedonian*. She was sent to the admiral; but what became of her, I never heard.

Before sending her away, however, the officers, having a peculiar itching for some of the brandy, took the liberty of replenishing their empty bottles from the hold. This, with true aristocratic liberality, they kept to themselves, without offering the smallest portion to the crew. Some of them showed, by their conduct afterwards, that this brandy possessed considerable strength. We had no further opportunity to signalize either ourselves or our frigate by our heroism at Brest; for we were soon after ordered back to Plymouth, where, for a short time, we lay at our old anchorage ground.

CHAPTER SIX

AT Plymouth we heard some vague rumors of a declaration of war against America. More than this, we could not learn, since the utmost care was taken to prevent our being fully informed. The reason of this secrecy was, probably, because we had several Americans in our crew, most of whom were pressed men, as before stated. These men, had they been certain that war had broken out, would have given themselves up as prisoners of war, and claimed exemption from that unjust service, which compelled them to act with the enemies of their country. This was a privilege which the magnanimity of our officers ought to have offered them. They had already perpetrated a grievous wrong upon them in impressing them; it was adding cruelty to injustice, to compel their service in a war against their own nation. But the difficulty with naval officers is, that they do not treat with a sailor as with a *man*. They know what is fitting between each other as officers; but they treat their crews on another principle; they are apt to look at them as pieces of living mechanism, born to serve, to obey their orders, and administer to their wishes without complaint. This is alike a bad morality and a bad philosophy. There is often more real manhood in the forecastle than in the ward-room; and until the common sailor is treated *as a man,* until every feeling of human nature is conceded to him in naval discipline—perfect, rational subordination will never be attained in ships of war, or in merchant vessels. It is needless to tell of the intellectual degradation of the mass of seamen. "A man's a man for a' that;" and it is this very system of discipline, this treating them as automatons, which keeps them degraded. When will human nature put more confidence in itself?

Leaving Plymouth, we next anchored, for a brief space, at Torbay, a small port in the British Channel. We were ordered thence to convoy a huge East India merchant vessel, much larger than our frigate, and having five hundred troops on board, bound to the East Indies, with money to pay the troops stationed there. We set sail in a tremendous gale of wind. Both ships stopped two days at Madeira to take in wine and a few other articles. After leaving this island, we kept her company two days more; and then, according to orders, having wished her success, we left her to pursue her voyage, while we returned to finish our cruise.

Though without any positive information, we now felt pretty certain that our government was at war with America. Among other things, our captain appeared more anxious than usual; he was on deck almost all the time; the "look-out" aloft was more rigidly observed; and every little while the cry of "Mast-head there!" arrested our attention.

It is customary in men of war to keep men at the fore and main mast-heads, whose duty it is to give notice of every new object that may appear. They are stationed on the royal yards, if they are up, but if not, on the top-gallant yards: at night a look-out is kept on the fore-yard only.

Thus we passed several days; the captain running up and down, and constantly hailing the man at the mast-head: early in the morning he began his charge "to keep a good look-out," and continued to repeat it until night. Indeed, he seemed almost crazy with some pressing anxiety. The men felt there was something anticipated, of which they were ignorant; and had the captain heard all their remarks upon his conduct, he would not have felt very highly flattered. Still, everything went on as usual; the day was spent in the ordinary duties of man-of-war life, and the evening in telling stories of things most rare and wonderful; for your genuine old tar is an adept in spinning yarns, and some of them, in respect to variety and length, might safely aspire to a place beside the great magician of the north, Sir Walter Scott, or any of those prolific heads that now bring forth such abundance of fiction to feed a greedy public, who read as eagerly as our men used to listen. To this yarn-spinning was added the most humorous singing, sometimes dashed with a streak of the pathetic, which I assure my readers was most touching; especially one very plaintive melody, with a chorus beginning with,

> Now if our ship should be east away,
> It would be our lot to see old England no more,

which made rather a melancholy impression on my boyish mind, and gave rise to a sort of presentiment that the *Macedonian* would never return home again; a presentiment which had its fulfillment in a manner totally unexpected to us all. The presence of a shark for several days, with its attendant pilot fish, tended to strengthen this prevalent idea.

The Sabbath came, and it brought with it a stiff breeze. We usually made a sort of holiday of this sacred day. After breakfast it was common to muster the entire crew on the spar deck, dressed as the fancy of the captain might dictate; sometimes in blue jackets and white trousers, or blue jackets and blue trousers; at other times in blue jackets, scarlet vests, and blue or white trousers; with our bright anchor buttons glancing in the sun, and our black, glossy hats, ornamented with black ribbons, and with the name of our ship painted on them. After muster, we frequently had church service read by the captain; the rest of the day was devoted to idleness. But we were destined to spend the Sabbath, just introduced to the reader, in a very different manner.

We had scarcely finished breakfast, before the man at the mast-head shouted, "Sail ho!"

The captain rushed upon deck, exclaiming, "Mast-head there!"

"Sir!"

"Where away is the sail? "

The precise answer to this question I do not recollect, but the captain proceeded to ask, "What does she look like? "

"A square-rigged vessel, sir," was the reply of the look-out.

After a few minutes, the captain shouted again, "Mast-head there!"

"Sir!"

"What does she look like?"

A large ship, sir, standing toward us!"

By this time, most of the crew were on deck, eagerly straining their eyes to obtain a glimpse of the approaching ship, and murmuring their opinions to each other on her probable character. Then came the voice of the captain, shouting, "Keep silence, fore and aft!" Silence being secured, he hailed the look-out, who, to his question of "What does she look like?" replied, "A large frigate, bearing down upon us, sir!"

A whisper ran along the crew that the stranger ship was a Yankee frigate. The thought was confirmed by the command of "All hands clear the ship for action, ahoy!" The drum and fife beat to quarters; bulk-heads were knocked away; the guns were released from their confinement; the whole dread paraphernalia of battle was produced; and after the lapse of a few minutes of hurry and confusion, every man and boy was at his post, ready to do his best service for his country, except the band, who, claiming exemption from the affray, safely stowed themselves away in the cable tier. We had only one sick man[1] on the list, and he, at the cry of battle, hurried from his cot, feeble as he was, to take his post of danger. A few of the junior midshipmen were stationed below, on the berth deck, with orders, given in our hearing, to shoot any man who attempted to run from his quarters.

Our men were all in good spirits; though they did not scruple to express the wish that the coming foe was a Frenchman rather than a Yankee. We had been told, by the Americans on board, that frigates in the American service carried more and heavier metal than ours. This, together with our consciousness of superiority over the French at sea, led us to a preference for a French antagonist.

The Americans among our number felt quite disconcerted, at the necessity which compelled them to fight against their own countrymen. One of them, named John Card, as brave a seaman as ever trod a plank, ventured to present himself to the captain, as a prisoner, frankly declaring his objections to fight. That officer, very ungenerously, ordered him to his quarters, threatening to shoot him if he made the request again. Poor fellow! He obeyed the unjust command, and was killed by a shot from his own countrymen. This fact is more disgraceful to the captain of the Macedonian, than even the loss of his ship. It was a gross and a palpable violation of the rights of man.

As the approaching ship showed American colors, all doubt of her character was at an end. "We must fight her," was the conviction of every breast. Every possible arrangement that could insure success, was accordingly made. The guns were shotted; the matches lighted; for, although our guns were all furnished with

---

[1] James Holmes, boatswain.

first-rate locks, they were also provided with matches, attached by lanyards, in case the lock should miss fire. A lieutenant then passed through the ship, directing the marines and boarders, who were furnished with pikes, cutlasses, and pistols, how to proceed if it should be necessary to board the enemy. He was followed by the captain, who extorted the men to fidelity and courage, urging upon their consideration the well-known motto of the brave Nelson, "England expects every man to do his duty." In addition to all these preparations on deck, some men were stationed in the tops with small-arms, whose duty it was to attend to trimming the sails, and to use their muskets, provided we came to close action. There were others also below, called sail trimmers, to assist in working the ship, should it be necessary to shift her position during the battle.

My station was at the fifth gun on the main deck. It was my duty to supply my gun with powder, a boy being appointed to each gun in the ship on the side we engaged, for this purpose. A woolen screen was placed before the entrance to the magazine, with a hole in it, through which the cartridges were passed to the boys; we received them there, and covering them with our jackets, hurried to our respective guns. These precautions are observed to prevent the powder taking fire before it reaches the gun.

Thus we all stood, awaiting orders, in motionless suspense. At last we fired three guns from the larboard side of the main deck; this was followed by the command, "Cease firing; you are throwing away your shot!"

Then came the order to "wear ship," and prepare to attack the enemy with our starboard guns. Soon after this I heard a firing from some other quarter, which I at first supposed to be a discharge from our quarter deck guns; though it proved to be the roar of the enemy's cannon.

A strange noise, such as I had never heard before, next arrested my attention; it sounded like the tearing of sails, just over our heads. This I soon ascertained to be the wind of the enemy's shot. The firing, after a few minutes' cessation, recommenced. The roaring of cannon could now be heard from all parts of our trembling ship, and, mingling as it did with that of our foes, it made a most hideous noise. By-and-by I heard the shot strike the sides of our ship; the whole scene grew indescribably confused and horrible; it was like some awfully tremendous thunder-storm, whose deafening roar is attended by incessant streaks of lightning, carrying death in every flash, and strewing the ground with the victims of its wrath: only, in our case, the scene was rendered more horrible than that, by the presence of torrents of blood which dyed our decks.

Though the recital may be painful, yet, as it will reveal the horrors of war, and show at what a fearful price a victory is won or lost, I will present the reader with things as they met my eye during the progress of this dreadful fight. I was busily supplying my gun with powder, when I saw blood suddenly fly from the arm of a man stationed at our gun. I saw nothing strike him; the effect alone was visible; in an instant, the third lieutenant tied his handkerchief round the wounded arm, and sent the groaning wretch below to the surgeon.

The cries of the wounded now rang through all parts of the ship. These were carried to the cockpit as fast as they fell, while those more fortunate men, who were killed outright, were immediately thrown overboard. As I was stationed but a short distance from the main hatchway, I could catch a glance at all who were carried below. A glance was all I could indulge in, for the boys belonging to the guns next to mine were wounded in the early part of the action, and I had to spring with all my might to keep three or four guns supplied with cartridges. I saw two of these lads fall nearly together. One of them was struck in the leg by a large shot; he had to suffer amputation above the wound. The other had a grape or canister shot sent through his ankle. A stout Yorkshireman lifted him in his arms, and hurried him to the cockpit. He had his foot cut off, and was thus made lame for life. Two of the boys stationed on the quarter deck were killed. They were both Portuguese. A man, who saw one of them killed, afterwards told me that his powder caught fire and burnt the flesh almost off his face. In this pitiable situation, the agonized boy lifted up both hands, as if imploring relief, when a passing shot instantly cut him in two.

I was an eye-witness to a sight equally revolting. A man named Aldrich had one of his hands cut off by a shot, and almost at the same moment he received another shot, which tore open his bowels in a terrible manner. As he fell, two or three men caught him in their arms, and, as he could not live, threw him overboard.

One of the officers in my division also fell in my sight. He was a noble-hearted fellow, named Nan Kivell.[1] A grape or canister shot

---

[1] James, in his *History of the British Navy*, gives this name as Thomas James; Nankivee.

struck him near the heart: exclaiming, "Oh! My God!" he fell, and was carried below, where he shortly after died.

Mr. Hope, our first lieutenant, was also slightly wounded by a grummet, or small iron ring, probably torn from a hammock clew by a shot. He went below, shouting to the men to fight on. Having had his wound dressed, he came up again, shouting to us at the top of his voice, and bidding us fight with all our might. There was not a man in the ship but would have rejoiced had he been in the place of our master's mate, the unfortunate Nan Kivell.

The battle went on. Our men kept cheering with all their might. I cheered with them, though I confess I scarcely knew for what. Certainly there was nothing very inspiriting in the aspect of things where I was stationed. So terrible had been the work of destruction round us, it was termed the slaughter-house. Not only had we had several boys and men killed or wounded, but several of the guns were disabled. The one I belonged to had a piece of the muzzle knocked out; and when the ship rolled, it struck a beam of the upper deck with such force as to become jammed and fixed in that position. A twenty-four pound shot had also passed through the screen of the magazine, immediately over the orifice through which we passed our powder. The schoolmaster[1] received a death wound. The brave boatswain, who came from the sick bay to the din of battle, was fastening a stopper on a back-stay which had been shot away, when his head was smashed to pieces by a cannon-ball; another man, going to complete the unfinished task, was also struck down. Another of our midshipmen also received a severe wound. The unfortunate ward-room steward, who, the reader will recollect, attempted to cut his throat on a former occasion, was killed. A fellow named John, who, for some petty offense, had been sent on board as a punishment, was carried past me, wounded. I distinctly heard the large blood-drops fall pat, pat, pat, on the deck; his wounds were mortal. Even a poor goat, kept by the officers for her milk, did not escape the general carnage; her hind legs were shot off, and poor Nan was thrown overboard.

Such was the terrible scene, amid which we kept on our shouting and firing. Our men fought like tigers. Some of them pulled off their jackets, others their jackets and vests; while some, still more determined, had taken off their shirts, and, with nothing but a handkerchief tied round the waistbands of their trousers, fought like heroes. Jack Sadler, whom the reader will recollect, was one of

---

[1] Dennis Colwell.

these. I also observed a boy, named Cooper, stationed at a gun some distance from the magazine. He came to and fro on the full run, and appeared to be as "merry as a cricket." The third lieutenant cheered him along, occasionally, by saying, "Well done, my boy, you are worth your weight in gold."

I have often been asked what were my feelings during this fight. I felt pretty much as I suppose every one does at such a time. That men are without thought when they stand amid the dying and the dead, is too absurd an idea to be entertained a moment. We all appeared cheerful, but I know that many a serious thought ran through my mind: still, what could we do but keep up a semblance, at least, of animation? To run from our quarters would have been certain death from the hands of our own officers; to give way to gloom, or to show fear, would do no good, and might brand us with the name of cowards, and ensure certain defeat. Our only true philosophy, therefore, was to make the best of our situation, by fighting bravely and cheerfully. I thought a great deal, however, of the other world; every groan, every falling man, told me that the next instant I might be before the Judge of all the earth. For this, I felt unprepared; but being without any particular knowledge of religious truth, I satisfied myself by repeating again and again the Lord's Prayer, and promising that if spared I would be more attentive to religious duties than ever before. This promise I had no doubt, at the time, of keeping; but I have learned since that it is easier to make promises amidst the roar of the battle's thunder, or in the horrors of shipwreck, than to keep them when danger is absent, and safety smiles upon our path.

While these thoughts secretly agitated my bosom, the din of battle continued. Grape and canister shot were pouring through our port-holes like leaden rain, carrying death in their trail. The large, shot came against the ship's side like iron hail, shaking her to the very keel, or passing through her timbers, and scattering terrific splinters, which did a more appalling work than even their own death-giving blows. The reader may form an idea of the effect of grape and canister, when he is told that grape shot is formed by seven or eight balls confined to an iron and tied in a cloth. These balls are scattered by the explosion of the powder. Canister shot is made by filling a powder canister with balls, each as large as two or three musket balls; these also scatter with direful effect when discharged. What then with splinters, cannon balls, grape and canister poured incessantly upon us, the reader may be assured that the work of death went on in a manner which must have been satisfactory even to the King of Terrors himself.

Suddenly, the rattling of the iron hail ceased. We were ordered to cease firing. A profound silence ensued, broken only by the stifled groans of the brave sufferers below. It was soon ascertained that the enemy had shot ahead to repair damages, for she was not so disabled but she could sail without difficulty; while we were so cut up that we lay utterly helpless. Our head braces were shot away; the fore and main top-masts were gone; the mizzen mast hung over the stern, having carried several men over in its fall: we were in the state of a complete wreck.

A council was now held among the officers on the quarter deck. Our condition was perilous in the extreme: victory or escape was alike hopeless. Our ship was disabled; many of our men were killed, and many more wounded. The enemy would without doubt bear down upon us in a few moments, and, as she could now choose her own position, would without doubt rake us fore and aft. Any further resistance was therefore folly. So, in spite of the hotbrained lieutenant, Mr. Hope, who advised them not to strike, but to sink alongside, it was determined to strike our bunting.[1] This was done by the hands of a brave fellow named Watson, whose saddened brow told how severely it pained his lion heart to do it. To me it was a pleasing sight, for I had seen fighting enough for one Sabbath; more than I wished to see again on a week day. His Britannic Majesty's frigate Macedonian was now the prize of the American frigate United States.

Before detailing the subsequent occurrences in my history, I will present the curious reader with a copy of Captain Carden's letter to the government, describing this action. It will serve to show how he excused himself for his defeat, as well as throw some light on those parts of the contest which were invisible to me at my station. My mother presented me with this document, on my return to England. She had received it from Lord Churchill, and had carefully preserved it for twenty years.

Admiralty Office, Dec. 29, 1812.

Copy of a letter from Captain John Surman Carden, late commander of His Majesty's ship the Macedonian,, to John

---

[1] The colors of the Macedonian are preserved at the Naval Institute, Annapolis, Md. A number of her cannon are placed on the green near the Commandant's quarters at the Brooklyn Navy Yard; and when she was broken up, many of her timbers were taken to City Island (now part of New York City), and used as the frame of a hotel still (1909) standing there.

Wilson Croker, Esq., dated on board the American ship United States, at sea, the 28th October, 1812:—

Sir: It is with the deepest regret, I have to acquaint you, for the information of my Lords Commissioners of the Admiralty, that His Majesty's late ship Macedonian was captured on the 25th instant, by the United States ship United States, Commodore Decatur commander. The detail is as follows:

A short time after daylight, steering N. W. by W., with the wind from the southward, in latitude 29° N., and longitude 29° 30' W., in the execution of their Lordships' orders, a sail was seen on the lee beam, which I immediately stood for, and made her out to be a large frigate, under American colors. At nine o'clock I closed with her, and she commenced the action, which we returned; but from the enemy keeping two points off the wind, I was not enabled to get as close to her as I could have wished. After an hour's action, the enemy backed and came to the wind, and I was then enabled to bring her to close battle. In this situation I soon found the enemy's force too superior to expect success, unless some very fortunate chance occurred in our favor; and with this hope

I continued the battle to two hours and ten minutes; when, having the mizzen mast shot away by the board, topmasts shot away by the caps, main yard shot in pieces, lower masts badly wounded, lower rigging all cut to pieces, a small proportion only of the fore-sail left to the fore-yard, all the guns on the quarter deck and forecastle disabled but two, and filled with wreck, two also on the main deck disabled, and several shot between wind and water, a very great proportion of the crew killed and wounded, and the enemy comparatively in good order, who had now shot ahead, and was about to place himself in a raking position, without our being enabled to return the fire, being a perfect wreck and unmanageable log; I deemed it prudent, though a painful extremity, to surrender His Majesty's ship; nor was this dreadful alternative resorted to till every hope of success was removed, even beyond the reach of chance; nor till, I trust their Lordships will be aware, every effort had been made against the enemy by myself, and my brave officers and men, nor should she have been surrendered whilst a man lived on board, had she been manageable. I am sorry to say our loss is very severe; I find by this day's muster, thirty-six killed, three of whom lingered a short time after the battle; thirty-six severely wounded, many of whom cannot recover, and thirty-two slightly wounded, who may all do well; total, one hundred and four.

The truly noble and animating conduct of my officers, and the steady bravery of my crew, to the last moment of the battle, must ever render them dear to their country.

My first lieutenant, David Hope, was severely wounded in the head, towards the close of the battle, and taken below; but was soon again on deck, displaying that greatness of mind and exertion, which, though it may be equalled, can never be excelled. The third lieutenant, John Bulford, was also wounded, but not obliged to quit his quarters; second lieutenant, Samuel Mottley, and he deserves my highest acknowledgments. The cool and steady conduct of Mr. Walker, the master, was very great during the battle, as also that of Lieutenants Wilson and Magill, of the marines.

On being taken on board the enemy's ship, I ceased to wonder at the result of the battle. The *United States* is built with the scantling of a seventy-four gun-ship, mounting thirty long twenty-four pounders (English ship-guns) on her main deck, and twenty-two forty-two pounders, carronades, with two long twenty-four pounders, on her quarter deck and forecastle, howitzer guns in her tops, and a traveling carronade on her upper deck, with a complement of four hundred and seventy-eight picked men.

The enemy has suffered much in masts, rigging, and hull, above and below water. Her loss in killed and wounded I am not aware of; but I know a lieutenant and six men have been thrown overboard.

Jno. S. Caeden.

To J. W. Crokeb, Esq., Admiralty.

Lord Churchill sent the above letter, with a list of the killed and wounded annexed, to inform my mother that the name of her son was not among the number. The act shows how much he could sympathize with a mother's feelings.

CHAPTER SEVEN

I NOW went below, to see how matters appeared there. The first object I met was a man bearing a limb, which had just been detached from some suffering wretch. Pursuing my way to the ward-room, I necessarily passed through the steerage, which was strewed with the wounded:[1] it was a sad spectacle, made more appalling by the groans and cries which rent the air. Some were groaning, others were swearing most bitterly, a few were praying, while those last arrived were begging most piteously to have their wounds dressed next. The surgeon and his mate were smeared with blood from head to foot: they looked more like butchers than doctors. Having so many patients, they had once shifted their

---

[1] The official report, from James' History of the British Navy, of the Macedonian's casualties was: David Hope, First Lieutenant, wounded, leg and head; John Bulford, Third Lieutenant, wounded; Henry Roebuck, Master's Mate, wounded; George Greenway, Midshipman, wounded; Francis Baker, "first-class volunteer," wounded.

Of the crew, 36 killed and 68 wounded, of whom two seamen died of wounds, and two boys had each one leg amputated. Nine Marines also were wounded.

Aboard the United States: Second Lieutenant John M. Funek, mortally wounded; one seaman mortally wounded; five seamen badly wounded.

(Unless the five all died, Captain Carden's statement in his official despatch home, "I saw a lieutenant and six seamen thrown overboard," was unfounded.

quarters from the cockpit to the steerage; they now removed to the ward-room, and the long table, round which the officers had sat over many a merry feast, was soon covered with the bleeding forms of maimed and mutilated seamen.

While looking round the ward-room, I heard a noise above, occasioned by the arrival of the boats from the conquering frigate. Very soon a lieutenant, I think his name was Nicholson,[1] came into the ward-room, and said to the busy surgeon, "How do you do, doctor? "

"I have enough to do," replied he, shaking his head thoughtfully; "you have made wretched work for us!" These officers were not strangers to each other, for the reader will recollect that the commanders and officers of these two frigates, had exchanged visits when we were lying at Norfolk, some months before.

I now set to work to render all the aid in my power to the sufferers. Our carpenter, named Reed, had his leg cut off. I helped to carry him to the after ward-room; but he soon breathed out his life there, and then I assisted in throwing his mangled remains overboard. We got out the cots as fast as possible; for most of them were stretched out on the gory deck. One poor fellow who lay with a broken thigh, begged me to give him water. I gave him some. He looked unutterable gratitude, drank, and died. It was with exceeding difficulty I moved through the steerage, it was so covered with mangled men, and so slippery with streams of blood. There was a poor boy there crying as if his heart would break. He had been servant to the bold boatswain, whose head was dashed to pieces. Poor boy! he felt that he had lost a friend. I tried to comfort him by reminding him that he ought to be thankful for having escaped death himself.

Here, also, I met one of my messmates, who showed the utmost joy at seeing me alive, for, he said, he had heard that I was killed. He was looking up his messmates, which he said was always done by sailors. We found two of our mess wounded. One was the Swede, Logholm, who fell overboard, as mentioned in a former chapter, and was nearly lost. We held him while the surgeon cut off his leg above the knee. The task was most painful to behold, the surgeon using his knife and saw on human flesh and bones, as freely as the butcher at the shambles does on the carcass of the beast! Our other messmate suffered still more than the Swede; he was sadly mutilated about the legs and thighs with splinters. Such

---

[1] John B. Nicholson.

scenes of suffering as I saw in that ward-room, I hope never to witness again. Could the civilized world behold them as they were, and as they often are, infinitely worse than, on that occasion, it seems to me they would forever put down the barbarous practices of war, by universal consent.

Most of our officers and men were taken on board the victor ship. I was left, with a few others, to take care of the wounded. My master, the sailing-master, was also among the officers, who continued in their ship. Most of the men who remained were unfit for any service, having broken into the spirit-room and made themselves drunk; some of them broke into the purser's room and helped themselves to clothing; while others, by previous agreement, took possession of their dead messmates' property. For my own part I was content to help myself to a little of the officers' provisions, which did me more good than could be obtained from rum. What was worse than all, however, was the folly of the sailors in giving spirit to their wounded messmates, since it only served to aggravate their distress.

Among the wounded, was a brave fellow named Wells. After the surgeon had amputated and dressed his arm, he walked about in fine spirits, as if he had received only a slight injury. Indeed, while under the operation, he manifested a similar heroism—observing to the surgeon, "I have lost my arm in the service of my country; but I don't mind it, doctor, it's the fortune of war." Cheerful and gay as he was, he soon died. His companions gave him rum; he was attacked by fever and died. Thus his messmates actually killed him with kindness.

We had all sorts of dispositions and temperaments among our crew. To me it was a matter of great interest to watch their various manifestations. Some who had lost their messmates appeared to care nothing about it, while others were grieving with all the tenderness of women. Of these, was the survivor of two seamen, who had formerly been soldiers in the same regiment; he bemoaned the loss of his comrade with expressions of profoundest grief. There were, also, two boatswain's mates, named Adams and Brown, who had been messmates for several years in the same ship. Brown was killed, or so wounded that he died soon after the battle. It was really a touching spectacle to see the rough, hardy features of the brave old sailor streaming with tears, as he picked out the dead body of his friend from among the wounded, and gently carried it to the ship's side, saying to the inanimate form he bore, "Oh Bill, we have sailed together in a number of ships, we have been in many gales and some battles, but this is the worst day I have seen! We must now part!" Here he dropped the body into the deep, and then, a fresh torrent of tears streaming over his weather-beaten face, he added, "I can do no more for you. Fare-well! God be with you!" Here was an instance of genuine friend-ship, worth more than the heartless professions of thousands, who, in the fancied superiority of their elevated position in the so-cial circle, will deign nothing but a silly sneer at this record of a sailor's grief.

The circumstance was rather a singular one, that in both the contending frigates the second boatswain's mate bore the name of William Brown, and that they both were killed; yet such was the fact.

The great number of the wounded kept our surgeon and his mate busily employed at their horrid work until late at night; and it was a long time before they had much leisure. I remember pass-ing round the ship the day after the battle. Coming to a hammock, I found some one in it apparently asleep. I spoke; he made no an-swer. I looked into the hammock; he was dead. My messmates coming up, we threw the corpse overboard; that was no time for useless ceremony. The man had probably crawled to his hammock the day before, and, not being perceived in the general distress, bled to death! Oh War! who can reveal thy miseries!

When the crew of the *United States* first boarded our frigate, to take possession of her as their prize, our men, heated with the fury of the battle, exasperated with the sight of their dead and wounded shipmates, and rendered furious by the rum they had obtained from the spirit-room, felt and exhibited some disposition to fight their captors. But after the confusion had subsided, and part of our men were snugly stowed away in the American ship, and the remainder found themselves kindly used in their own, the utmost good feeling began to prevail. We took hold and cleansed the ship, using hot vinegar to take out the scent of the blood that had dyed the white of our planks with crimson. We also took hold and aided in fitting our disabled frigate for her voyage. This being accomplished, both ships sailed in company toward the American coast.

I soon felt myself perfectly at home with the American seamen; so much so, that I chose to mess with them. My shipmates also participated in similar feelings in both ships. All idea that we had been trying to shoot out each other's brains so shortly before, seemed forgotten. We eat together, drank together, joked, sung, laughed, told yarns; in short, a perfect union of ideas, feelings, and purposes, seemed to exist among all hands.

A corresponding state of unanimity existed, I was told, among the officers. Commodore Decatur showed himself to be a gentleman as well as a hero in his treatment of the officers of the *Macedonian*. When Captain Carden offered his sword to the commodore, remarking, as he did so, "I am an undone man. I am the first British naval officer that has struck his flag to an American." The noble commodore either refused to receive the sword, or immediately returned it, smiling as he said, "You are mistaken, sir; your *Guerriere* has been taken by us, and the flag of a frigate thus was struck before yours."[1] This somewhat revived the spirits of the old captain; but, no doubt, he still felt his soul stung with shame and mortification at the loss of his ship. Participating as he did in the haughty spirit of the British aristocracy, it was natural for him to feel galled and wounded to the quick, in the position of a conquered man.

We were now making the best of our way to America. Notwithstanding the patched-up condition of the *Macedonian?*[1] she was far superior, in a sailing capacity, to her conqueror. The *United States* had always been a dull sailer, and had been christened by the name of the Old Wagon. Whenever a boat came alongside of our frigate, and the boatswain's mate was ordered to "pipe away" the boat's crew, he used to sound his shrill call on the whistle, and bawl out, "Away, Wagoners, away," instead of "away, *United States* men, away." This piece of pleasantry used to be rebuked by the officers, but in a manner that showed they enjoyed the joke. They usually replied, "Boatswain's mate, you rascal, pipe away *United States* men, not Wagoners. We have no wagoners on board of a ship." Still, in spite of rebuke, the joke went on, until it grew stale by repetition. One thing was made certain however by the sailing qualities of the *Macedonian;* which was, that if we had been disposed to escape from our foe before the action, we could have done so with all imaginable ease. This, however, would have justly exposed us to disgrace, while our capture did not.

There was every reason why the *United States* should beat us. She was larger in size, heavier in metal, more numerous in men,

---

[1] The Guerriere was the first frigate captured, the Frolic (taken October 18) being a brig.— (Ed.)

The first lieutenant of the United States, William H. Allen, took the Macedonian to port. The list of the United States' officers and their subsequent careers is placed in Appendix A.

and stronger built than the *Macedonian*. Another fact in her favor was, that our captain at first mistook her for the *Essex*, which carried short carronades, hence he engaged her at long shot at first; for, as we had the weather gage, we could take what position we pleased. But this maneuver only wasted our shot, and gave her the advantage, as she actually carried larger metal than we did. When we came to close action, the shot from the *United States* went through and through our ship, while ours struck her sides, and fell harmlessly into the water. This is to be accounted for both by the superiority of the metal and of the ship. Her guns were heavier and her sides thicker than ours. Some have said that her sides were stuffed with cork. Of this, however, I am not certain. Her superiority, both in number of men and guns, may easily be seen by the following statistics. We carried forty-nine guns; long eighteen-pounders on the main deck, and thirty-two pound carronades on the quarter deck and forecastle. Our whole number of hands, including officers, men and boys, was three hundred. The *United States* carried four hundred and fifty men and fifty-four guns: long twenty-four pounders on the main deck, and forty-two pound carronades on the quarter deck and forecastle. So that in actual force she was immensely our superior.

To these should be added the consideration that the men in the two ships fought under the influence of different motives. Many of our hands were in the service against their will; some of them were Americans, wrongfully impressed, and inwardly hoping for defeat: while nearly every man in our ship sympathized with the great principle for which the American nation so nobly contended in the war of 1812. What that was, I suppose all my readers understand. The British, at war with France, had denied the Americans the right to trade thither. She had impressed American seamen, and forcibly compelled their service in her navy; she had violated the American flag by insolently searching their vessels for her runaway seamen. Free trade and sailors' rights, therefore, were the objects contended for by the Americans. With these objects our *men* could but sympathize, whatever our officers might do.

On the other hand, the crew of our opponent had all shipped *voluntarily* for the term of two years only; (most of our men were shipped for life.) They understood what they fought for; they were better used in the service. What wonder, then, that victory adorned the brows of the American commander? To have been defeated under such circumstances would have been a source of lasting infamy to any naval officer in the world. In the matter of fighting, I think there is but little difference in either nation. Place them in action under equal circumstances and motives, and who could predict which would be victor? Unite them together, they would subject the whole world. So close are the alliances of blood, however, between England and America, that it is to be earnestly desired, they may never meet in mortal strife again. If either will fight, which is to be deprecated as a crime and a folly, let it choose an enemy less connected by the sacred ties of consanguinity.

Our voyage was one of considerable excitement. The seas swarmed with British cruisers, and it was extremely doubtful whether the *United States* would elude their grasp, and reach the protection of an American port with her prize. I hoped most sincerely to avoid them, as did most of my old shipmates; in this we agreed with our captors, who wisely desired to dispose of one conquest before they attempted another. Our former officers, of course, were anxious for the sight of a British flag. But we saw none, and, after a prosperous voyage from the scene of conflict, we heard the welcome cry of "Land ho!" The *United States* entered the port of New London; but, owing to a sudden shift of the wind, the *Macedonian* had to lay off and on for several hours. Had an English cruiser found us in this situation, we should have been easily recovered; and, as it was extremely probable we .should fall in with one, I felt quite uneasy, until, after several hours, we made out to run into the pretty harbor of Newport. We fired a salute as we came to an anchor, which was promptly returned by the people on shore.

With a few exceptions, our wounded men were in a fair way to recover by the time we reached Newport. The last of them, who died of their wounds on board, was buried just before we got in. His name was Thomas Whittaker; he had been badly wounded by splinters. While he lived, he endured excessive torture. At last his sufferings rendered him crazy, in which sad state he died. He was sewed up in his hammock, by his messmates, and carried on a grating to the larboard bow port. There Mr. Archer, a midshipman of the *Macedonian,* read the beautiful burial service of the church of England. When he came to that most touching passage, "we commit the body of our brother to the deep," the grating was elevated, and, amid the most profound silence, the body fell heavily into the waters. As it dropped into the deep, a sigh escaped from many a friendly bosom, and an air of passing melancholy shrouded many a face with sadness. Old recollections were busy there, calling up the losses of the battle; but it was only momentary. The men brushed away their tears, muttered" It's no use to fret," and things once more wore their wonted aspect.

At Newport our wounded were carried on shore. Our former officers also left us here. When my master, Mr. Walker, took his leave of me, he appeared deeply affected. Imprinting a kiss on my cheek, the tears started from his eyes, and he bade me adieu. I have not seen him since.

While we lay here, a few days, several of our men contrived to run away. I should have done so too, but for the vigilance of the prize officers, who were ordered to keep us, that we might be exchanged for those Americans who had fallen into British hands.

After staying a short time in this port, we got under weigh and ran into New London. Here we fired a gun as a signal; it was answered by the *United States,* and both ships were presently sailing in company to New York. We found the Sound plentifully dotted with sloops, carrying passengers, for this was before the days of modern steam boating. After we reached Hurl-gate, vessels here gave us plenty of employment. Most of them honored us with three cheers, as they passed. Of course, the prize crew could do no less than cheer again, so that we passed our time amidst continued cheering. While here, we were favored with abundant visitors, curious to see the captive frigate. Finding these visitors extremely inquisitive, and being tolerably good-natured myself, I found a profitable business in conducting them about the ship, describing the action, and pointing out the places where particular individuals fell. For these services, I gained some money and more good will. The people who had been to see us, used to tell on shore how they had been on board of us, and how the English boy had conducted them over the ship, and told them the particulars of the fight. It soon became quite common for those who came to inquire "if I was the English boy that was taken in her." This civility on my part was not without a motive; it was productive of profit, and I wanted money to aid me whenever I got clear, which I was fully determined to do, the first opportunity.

To this step I was encouraged by our pilot, who brought us from New London, Mr. Tinker. He promised to take me as his apprentice, if I ran away. Also a gentleman who visited us told me to call at his house in Pearl street, and he would give me a dinner. Many others advised me to get away if possible. But I was so closely watched that my mind was haunted with fear, lest, after all, I should be sent back to England in the Cartel, which was expected every day for the release of the prisoners. To fail in the attempt, exposed me to the danger of being reported to the officer who might come for us, and thus I was liable to be flogged whenever I arrived in a British port. Great caution was therefore necessary in making the effort; since it was better not to try at all, than to fail of success.

Christmas was now drawing near. The day before Christmas day, the Americans contrived to get well supplied with wine from a barrel they found below. As they had no funds, I bought my messmates some apples and a turkey, so that on the morrow they were quite taken up with feasting. We also had a great many visitors that day; many of them were ladies, and the officers got a chair out, which Captain Carden had rigged up, to lift ladies on board. It was made from an old hogshead, in the following manner. One head was knocked out and the barrel scooped out in front; a seat was then inserted, with a flag thrown over the whole; so that when it was lowered into a boat alongside, the lady had but to step in and throw the flag round her feet; in a trice, the chair was whipped upon deck by the halyards, when the lady could step out with perfect ease. This contrivance afforded a great deal of amusement, and kept the officers busily occupied in waiting upon their lady visitors. Now then, thought I, is my time for escape, or not at all. I had already made a friend of the American boatswain, Mr. Dawson, who promised to carry my clothes to New York, if I got clear. So, looking over the ship's side, I saw a small colored boy in a boat. "Can you tell me," said I, hailing him, "where I can get some geese and turkeys on shore for our officers?"

"I guess you can at some of the houses," responded the lad.

"Well, then," I continued, "will you set me ashore? I want to get some for our officers."

To this he replied, "Yes, if you will go and ask my master, who is on board your ship."

This was a damper on my young hopes, since it was not likely that his master would give permission. I went below, somewhat disconcerted. There I met a boy named James Day, two years younger than myself. I told him I was going to run away, and urged him to go with me. He declined at first, saying, "I have no money to pay my expenses."

"But I have money," returned I, "and as long as I have a shilling, you shall have half of it."

"Besides," continued he, "I am afraid we cannot get away without being caught, and so get a thorough flogging."

"Never mind that," said I; "I have contrived that business. The boat's waiting to set us ashore. Come along, Jim; don't be frightened; 'Nothing venture, nothing have,' you know. Come, come, here's the boat alongside." At length he consented; we returned to the ship's side, and told the boy his master was willing, provided he would make haste. We jumped into the boat, and were soon hurrying towards the shore, full of the hope of freedom.

Never did my heart misgive me as it did when we were on our way to the shore; the voice of the boy's master came echoing along the waves. "Where are you going with that boat?" he shouted. Recovering myself, I persuaded the boy he was only bidding him to make haste. So the lad replied, "I am going to get some geese, sir!" and pulled on. A few minutes more, and, to my unspeakable delight, I stood on American soil. Giving the boy a half dollar, we pushed on for New York, some ten miles distant.

For this act of running away, I have never blamed myself; for the means by which it was effected, I have frequently done so. As the reader has seen, it was done at the expense of truth. I told several deliberate lies to the deceived boy in the boat. This is inexcusable, and the only palliation that can be offered is, my want of religious instruction. I was not then a Christian. Still, the act of lying was an offense before God, and no man should purchase his liberty at the price of a lie. He who saves his life at the cost of offending God, pays dearly for the purchase. I am thankful I have since learned this lesson, at the foot of the cross of Jesus Christ.

Not having our "land legs" on, we soon became excessively fatigued. When within two or three miles of the city, we concluded to stop all night at a tavern on the road.

The inmates looked somewhat surprised to see two sailor lads inquiring for lodgings; so I at once told them we were runaways from the captured frigate. This made them our friends! The evening passed quite pleasantly; we relating the particulars of the battle, and singing sea songs, and they listening with the utmost good humor.

It seemed strange to us to find ourselves in a bed, after sleeping two years and a half in a hammock; nevertheless, we slept soundly, and to our inexpressible pleasure arose in the morning at our leisure, without being driven by the swearing boatswain at our heels. After breakfast, our generous host having refused to receive any payment for his hospitality, we set out for the city of New York.

Here I very fortunately alighted on one of the crew of the *Macedonian,* named Fitzgibbons, who informed me that most of our men had been landed at New London, and confined as prisoners in

SAMUEL LEECH

an old barn; but that, not being over closely guarded, most of them
had run away. He also introduced me to a sailors' boarding-house,
kept by a widow named Elms, near the old Fly Market in Front
street.

After spending a week in roving about the city, I heard a tremendous roaring of cannon in the harbor; it proceeded from the
two frigates—which had dropped down from Hurl-gate and hauled
up off the navy yard. What was more to my satisfaction, however,
was the news that the Cartel had arrived and carried off the British
crew, or, rather, the fragment that remained of them. Had I delayed my escape three days longer, instead of spending the rest of
my days in America and in the American service, I should have
been chained to the obnoxious discipline of the British navy. The
reader may be assured that the narrowness of my escape very
greatly enhanced the value I set upon my freedom.

I now ventured on board the *Macedonian* again to obtain my
clothes. As I stepped on board, my mind misgave me, as Lieutenant Nicholson eyed me somewhat sternly; but I was reassured,
when, kindly speaking, he informed me that the Cartel was gone,
and I was safe. The sailors, also, congratulated me on my success
in getting clear.

The officers and crew were about to have a public dinner, and
to visit the theatre in commemoration of their achievement. The
sailors invited me to join them. To this I agreed. But overhauling
my clothes, and contriving how I should appear as well as any
shipmates, who were all going to have new suits for the occasion,
the bright anchor buttons, which shone on my best suit, presented
an insuperable objection. For how could I appear among them
with the badge of the British service on my coat? This dilemma
was removed, however, by the skill of my landlady, the widow,
who very carefully covered the buttons with blue cloth.

There was great excitement in New York, when the brave tars
of the victorious *United States,* walked in triumphant procession
through the streets, in the presence of countless citizens. First,
came Captain Carden's band, which had now shipped with Decatur; they were followed by the commodore and his officers, and
these by the crew. At the City Hotel, all hands partook of a sump-
tuous dinner. This was followed by rather more than a usual
amount of drinking, laughing, and talking; for as liquor was furnished in great abundance, the men could not resist the temptation to get drunk. As they left the room to go to the theatre, the
poor plates on the sideboard proclaimed that "Jack was full three

sheets in the wind." Almost every one, as he passed, gave them a crack, crying out as they fell, "Save the pieces;" thus illustrating the old proverb, "When rum is in, wit is out."

The visit to the theatre passed off very much like the dinner, to wit, there was an abundance of shouting and cheering all the evening. After the close of the play, all hands scattered to see their friends, with orders to be on board next day. It was a week before they all returned.

I was much struck with the appearance of Decatur that evening, as he sat in full uniform, his pleasant face flushed with the excitement of the occasion. He formed a striking contrast to the appearance he made when he visited our ship on the passage to New York. Then, he wore an old straw hat and a plain suit of clothes, which made him look more like a farmer than a naval commander.

Never had men more friends than the crew of the *United States* at this period. Every boarding-house was open to them; every merchant would trust them; every one was willing to lend them money. What was it that gained them such public favor? "Oh their victory, of course," replies the reader. Stop; I will reveal the secret. They had some prize money coming to them in a few weeks! That was the key that unlocked coffers; the warmth that melted the heart; the spirit that clothed the face with smiles. But for that—the prize money—poor Jack's credit and favor would, as usual, have been below *par*.

Of course, this profusion, this universal popularity, almost turned the brains of some of those old tars; and at every opportunity they would steal ashore for a spree. This brought them into trouble; it brought some of them to the gangway to be flogged. These floggings, however, were not very severe; they were rather a species of farce, enacted to preserve alive the forms of discipline. To avoid even these forms, the men were accustomed, after staying on a spree for several days, to visit the commodore's lady, with some piteous tale, begging her to intercede for them with their captain. This she did with almost constant success. The lucky tar would then go on board, telling his messmates that she was the sailor's friend, and using the usual saying in such cases, "Good luck to her —she has a soul to be saved."

By this time, the late crew of the *Macedonian,* or those of them who had not gone home with the Cartel, were pretty well scattered over the country. One of the marines, named Luke Oil, went to Springfield, Mass., where he was employed as a file-cutter by

SAMUEL LEECH

Colonel Lee, of the U. S. armory, at the rate of $75 per month. This prosperity, and an unfortunate marriage, led him into unsteady habits. He enlisted into the U. S. Army; but growing sick of that, Colonel Lee procured his discharge. He afterwards enlisted again, which is the last I ever heard of Luke Oil. Two more of our marines, named Shipley and Taylor, also went to Springfield, and were employed by a Mr. Ames.

Several of the others enlisted to serve in the fort at New London. One of these, whose name was Hawkins, was very highly esteemed for his excellence as a soldier, and was soon made sergeant. But being an inveterate drunkard, he lost his office, and was degraded to the ranks.

I have a characteristic anecdote to record of Sadler, the messmate of Bob Hammond. He enlisted in the American army, and was quartered at Hartford. He was so delighted with everything American, that he had grown to be an enthusiast in his encomiums on the government, as was exhibited one day in a somewhat peculiar way. The company to which he belonged was marched to church, one Sabbath, to hear (I think it was) priest Strong.[1] The text was, "Fear God and honor the king." This was too much for the newly-made American; and he put the congregation into a broad grin, by exclaiming aloud, "Don't let us hear about the King, but about Congress." The good people of Hartford would have pardoned this violation of Puritan propriety, if they had seen that brave fellow flogged, as I had, in the king's service.

Our fifer, Charles Robinson, also enlisted in the same regiment. Perhaps some of the inhabitants of Hartford still remember the soldier who amused them, during his stay, by playing on the bugle in the morning, from the top of the court-house. Robinson was perfect master of several instruments, especially the fife and the bugle.

One of our boys, named William Madden, but better known in the *Macedonian* by the nick-name of "Billy O'Rook," from his practice of singing a song about that hero, enlisted in the army, and afterwards performed a signal service for his adopted country, at Sacket's Harbor. The Americans were in full retreat before the

[1] This was the celebrated Dr. Nathan Strong (1748-1816), pastor of the First Congregational Church.

British troops, whose general,[1] mounted on a superb charger, was at their head, shouting, "Huzza, my boys, the day is ours!" when young Madden rendered desperate by the certainty of being shot, if taken by his countrymen, deliberately aimed his rifle at the general. The shot struck him, he fell, and the British retreated. This brave lad lost his life in a subsequent action. I make this statement on the authority of Captain Badger, of Williamstown, Mass., confirmed by the testimony of several other persons.

The reader has probably not forgotten the name of "Bloody Dick." He shipped on board the *Hornet,* sloop of war, and with that vessel very narrowly escaped falling into the hands of the English. I met him afterwards in New York. He told me how he trembled during the chase, knowing that if captured he should be hung for entering the American service; the British having given express orders for a strict look-out after our crew, that they might make examples of them.

Besides the men just mentioned, others of our crew shipped and wandered in every direction; some in men of war, some in merchant vessels; some, fearful of the risk of being retaken, settled ashore. In short, it is impossible to trace them, so variously did they diverge from each other. I have been particular in mentioning the history of a few, to gratify the parties, should they be living, and ever see my book; to confirm the reader in the truthfulness of my account, and to show some of the changes that followed in consequence of the victory of the *United States* over the *Macedonian.* It would be an interesting task, were it possible, to trace out all the results of that victory. Having detained the reader thus long in following the fate of my shipmates, I will resume the record of my own in the following chapter.

---

[1] This was Captain Grey, the adjutant-general, son of General Sir Charles Grey, of the Paoli massacre, September, 1777- Lossing (Field-Book War of 1812) says a drummer-boy cried, "Perhaps not yet," fired, and mortally wounded him.

CHAPTER EIGHT

NEARLY two weeks had passed since I left the *Macedonian*. I and my companion were living upon the sums I had saved from the presents I received for my civilities to her numerous visitors. One day, as I was sauntering round the wharves, with my protege, I met a number of men-of-war's men. Stepping up to them, I perceived some of the old *Macedonians*. Of course, I hailed them. They were glad to see me. They had shipped on board the *John Adams,* guard ship, to which they were returning, having been enjoying a few days' liberty. Nothing would satisfy them, but for us to accompany them, and ship too. The midshipman who was with them, joined his entreaties to theirs, and we at last consented.

To avoid being detected by the British, it was usual for our men to assume new names, and to hail from some American port, on shipping in an American vessel. My shipmates advised me to do the same. To this I had some objections, because I knew that changing my name would not make me a Yankee, while it might bring me into as awkward a position as it did an Irishman, who was found by an English cruiser on board an American vessel. After he had declared himself an American, the officer asked him, "What part of America did you come from?"

"I used to belong to Philamadelph, but now I belong to Philama York," replied Paddy, concealing his brogue as much as possible. "Well," continued the officer, "can you say pease?"

"Pase, sir," said Pat in true Irish style. The officer laughed and replied, "Mr. Pase, you will please to get into the boat." The poor Irishman was unsuccessful in playing the Yankee.

Mentioning these fears, the midshipman said, "Call yourself William Harper, and hail from Philadelphia;" then turning to my companion, he added, "and call yourself James Wilson."

"But," said I, "suppose the officer should ask any questions about Philadelphia, what should I do? "

"Oh say you belong to Pine street."

"But what if he asks me in what part of the city Pine street is situated, and what streets join it?" I answered, determined not to take a step in the dark if I could avoid it.

The midshipman assured me that no such questions would be put; and, partly confiding and partly doubting, I resolved to make the experiment. Going on board, we were paraded before the officers. Addressing me, one of them said, "Well, my boy, what is your name?"

Mustering all the confidence I could command, I boldly answered, "William Harper, sir."

"What part of America do you belong to, my boy?"

"Philadelphia, sir."

Here one of the officers smiled and remarked, "Ah, a townsman." I trembled at hearing this, inwardly hoping that they would ask me no more questions. To my increased alarm, however, he continued by asking, "What street in Philadelphia? "

"Pine street, sir," said I, with the air of a man who feels himself drawn toward a crisis he cannot escape.

"What street joins Pine street, my lad?" asked my tormentor, with a knowing laugh.

This was a poser; for further than this my instructions had not proceeded. However, I rallied the little confidence which remained, and said, "I don't remember, sir."

The officer who had claimed me as a townsman, mentioned the next street, and my examiner went on by asking me what street joined the one mentioned by the officer.

My colors, which had fallen to half-mast before, were now fairly struck. I had to surrender at discretion; but thinking to get off with the honors of war, I answered, "Gentlemen, it is so long since I was in Philadelphia, I have forgotten all about it."

This point blank shot might have saved me, when, as if Providence had determined to make my attempt at lying a total failure, one of them detected a glittering anchor button, which had contrived to get rid of the covering placed over it by the fingers of the widow. Pointing it out to the others, he said, "Where did you get that English button? Did you pick it up in Philadelphia?"

This was a shot which raked me fore and aft. I hauled down my colors and stood silent. The officers laughed heartily as one of them said, "Go below, my lad; you will make a pretty good Yankee."

Through all this procedure the reader will perceive how perfect was the disregard of truth among all parties, from my humble self to the officers, who were evidently rather pleased than otherwise at my attempt to pass for an American. Such an absence of moral rectitude is deplorable; it exhibits the unfitness of the parties for a mansion in His kingdom who is a God of truth: it lays the foundation for a mutual distrust and suspicion among men, and it leaves the offender to meet a fearful weight of responsibility in the day that shall try every man's work. I am thankful that the influences of Christianity have fallen upon me since that time, in such abundance as to renew the spirit of my mind, and to fill me with abhorrence towards a violation of truth.

The next morning I and my companion, who had escaped the ordeal that had proved too much for me, were summoned to go ashore to the rendezvous, that we might sign the ship's articles; or, in sailor phrase, get shipped. The officer of the watch shouted, "Boatswain's mate!"

"Sir," answered a deep, gruff voice.

"Pipe away the cutter," said the officer.

"Aye, aye, sir."

"Pass the word for James Wilson and William Harper."

"Aye, aye, sir."

Then followed a loud, shrill whistle, accompanied with the cry of, "Away, there, cutters, away!" We were also summoned to appear, and told to take our seats in the cutter, which by this time lay alongside, manned by her crew of six men, who sat each with his oar elevated in the air, waiting the word of command. We were soon seated, the lieutenant passed the words, "Let fall, and give way;" the oars fell into the water with admirable precision, and away we flew towards the shore.

On our way to the rendezvous, I told my companion I should not ship in the *John Adams*, because so many of the *Macedonians* were already there, and it was impossible for us to pass for Americans. After some debate, we agreed together not to sign the articles. On entering the house where the stars and stripes were flying over the door, in token of its being the naval rendezvous, being anxious to have my friend Wilson pass the ordeal first, I affected to stumble, and then continued apparently engaged in fixing my shoe-string. "Well, my boy, what is your name? Just sign it here, will you?" said the officer.

I took no notice, but remained very busy with my shoes. My shipmate replied in a low, bashful voice, "I don't like to ship, sir."

"Very well, then go below," said the officer. At this juncture, feeling encouraged by his remark, I looked up; when, to my discomfiture, the officer, fixing his eyes on my retreating companion, observed, "That fellow will certainly be hung;" meaning that he would get caught by the English. Then, addressing me, he said, "Now, my lad, just sign your name."

"Sir," said I, "I had better not ship alone. The other boy is only frightened; let me talk to him a little, and I can persuade him to ship with me."

The shipping officer was too old a bird to be snared with such chaff as this. So, speaking rather sharply, he said, "Let him go, sir, and ship yourself; then he'll come back and join you; and "— he smiled as he spoke—" I will let you come ashore to persuade him, in a day or two."

Still I pretended not to be convinced, and, after considerable debate, he let me off. Once more clear, I joined my young shipmate, and we proceeded together to our boarding-house, congratulating ourselves on our fortunate escape, as it appeared to us.

Two weeks of idleness had nearly exhausted the little stock of funds I had picked up on board my old ship, and it was becoming necessary for me to find some means or other of supporting myself; for although the prim widow, with whom I boarded, was quite obliging while her bills were paid, it was altogether probable that she would become a little crusty if they should be neglected. At this crisis I fortunately met with an Englishman, who had visited our frigate at Hurl-gate. His name was Smith; he was a deserter from the British army; but was now settled in New York, as a bootmaker, in the employment of the firm of Benton & Co., Broadway. He offered to take me and initiate me into the art, science and secrets of boot-making. Seeing no better opportunity before me, I accepted his kind offer, and at once entered on my novitiate.

Behold me then, kind reader, transformed from the character of a runaway British sailor, into that of a quiet scholar, at the feet of St. Crispin, where in the matter of awls, wax-ends, lapstones and pegs, I soon became quite proficient.

It is altogether probable that the rest of my life would have glided away in this still and quiet manner, but for a report that reached me, one Sabbath, as I was wasting its precious hours in wandering about among the shipping. This was, that there was a tall, stout seaman on board the *United States,* named George Turner. From the name and description, I had no doubt that this was my cousin, who (the reader has not forgotten I presume) presented himself so unceremoniously to my aunt at Wanstead.

This intelligence determined me to pay that frigate a visit. Going on board, I found her crew living in a complete Elysium of sensual enjoyment. They had recently received their prize money. Salt beef and pork were now rejected with disdain: Jack's messkids smoked with more savory viands, such as soft tack (bread) and butter, fried eggs, sausages, etc.; the whole well soaked with copious streams of rum and brandy.

Those of the crew who had been in the *Macedonian,* hailed me with a hearty welcome; those for whom I had bought the turkey and apples at Christmas repaid me fourfold, so that when I went ashore that night my purse was as heavy as on the afternoon when I quitted my ship. My cousin did not recognize me at first; but by referring him to his visit to my old abode, he at last felt satisfied that I was his cousin. He then charged me not to mention our relationship, because he wished to pass for an American. Having given me this charge, he surveyed me from head to foot, and then said, "What are you doing in New York? "

"I am learning to make boots and shoes."

"I am sorry you are bound to a shoemaker," said he; "I don't like that business."

"I am not *bound* to Mr. Smith, but can leave him when I please."

"Well, then," he remarked thoughtfully, "I don't want you to go to sea again. Go to Salem, in the state of Massachusetts. I have a wife and children there, and shall be at home in a few weeks."

This was a kind offer, and I at once agreed to take his advice. I had already grown somewhat weary with the confinement of my new mode of life, though, on the whole, considering my education, and the character of the influence exerted upon me in the *Mace-*

donian, I was a steady lad. Mr. Smith had left me pretty much to my own inclinations during the two months of my residence with him; yet my utmost misconduct had been the drinking of a little spirit, and the violation of the Sabbath by roaming about the docks and wharves. My Sabbath evenings I had usually spent in a more profitable manner, it being my habit to spend them at the Methodist chapel in Duane street.

On returning to the house of my kind employer, I lost no time in communicating to him my change of purpose. He objected, and justly too, to be left just as the pains he had taken to instruct me were about to be requited by my usefulness. However, as I offered him five dollars, he consented to my departure.

At that time there were no steamboats ploughing the waters of the Sound, so I engaged a steerage passage to Providence, for five dollars, on board a packet sloop, and, with a light heart and elastic step, carried my clothes-bag on board. Here, however, I met with a trifling loss. While ashore waiting for a fair wind, a negro, who had engaged a passage in the sloop, robbed my bag of several articles of wearing apparel, and took French leave. In consideration of this mishap, the captain exacted only three dollars passage-money. From Providence a stage, chartered exclusively by a party of sailors, conveyed me to Boston; from whence I soon reached the house of my cousin in Salem.

Mrs. Turner received me with great kindness; indeed, she pretended not to be surprised at my visit, assigning as a reason the very satisfactory fact that she had seen me with my bag on my shoulder in the *grounds of a teacup!* She was a believer in fortune telling and dreams, having, for aught I know, received her convictions as an heirloom from her witch-burning[1] ancestors. At any rate she was strongly confirmed in her favorite theory by my timely arrival; verifying, as it did, to the very particular of the bag on the shoulder, the truth-telling tea-grounds.

She gave me another proof, after I had been there a few weeks, of the truthfulness and verity of dreams, by calling me up one

---

[1] Leech is not to be blamed for his belief in the burning of witches in New England—in 1909 a New York orator repeated the same hoary blunder. -(Ed.)

[Expansion] Between February 1692 and May 1693 approximately 150 people were arrested and accused of witchcraft in Essex, Suffolk, and Middlesex Counties of Massachusetts. Of these, 29 people were convicted; and of these, 19 were hanged (14 women and five men). No one was burned. [Fireship Press Editor] morning, with an injunction to make haste to the post-office, for she had dreamed of catching fish. Sure enough, if she caught no fish in her dreams, she caught a very fine one in the letter I brought to her, for it contained a one hundred dollar bill from her husband, with information that his ship was blockaded in the port of New London by Commodore Hardy.

Accident or curiosity, I forget which, led me to attend the religious services of the Baptists in Salem. They were enjoying a season of religious refreshing: several were baptized. The hymn beginning with the line—

Oh, how happy are they who their Savior obey,

was sung as the converts came out of the water, and made a strong impression on my mind. Had some devoted Christian made himself acquainted with my feelings, and given me suitable advice, there is no doubt but that I should have been led to embrace the Lord Jesus Christ. How many divine impressions are destroyed, through lack of faithfulness in Christians!

Perhaps the great reason why these serious impressions were so transient, was because the company I kept was so unfavorable to their growth. Most of my time was spent about the shipping: among these were many privateers, the profanity of whose crews was such that it had passed into a proverb. It was usual to say to a gross swearer, "You swear like a privateer's-man." Religion could not flourish in an atmosphere tainted by their vices.

Among my favorite pursuits was that of fishing. Sometimes I went with mixed parties of males and females; at others, with a few sailor companions. One of these excursions came very near costing rather more than it was worth. We had been out all night; towards morning we thought we would get a little sleep, and for this purpose laid ourselves down under the top-gallant forecastle. Luckily for us, we had an old sailor, named Lewis Deal, on board. He had been quartermaster on board the *United States*. Knowing that the coast was strictly guarded by British cruisers, he kept awake. Just at dawn the *bang* of a single gun led him to call us, saying, "There, I told you to look out for Johnny Bull."

Looking about us, we saw an English gun brig in chase after a Boston sloop. This was a sight that inspired us with a very sudden and wonderful agility, since we had a decided repugnance to a free passage in the aforesaid brig to Halifax; especially as in my case it might have the rather unpleasant termination of an airing at the yard-arm; which, for very strong reasons I chose to avoid if possible.

By dint of strong arms and quick movements, we succeeded in hauling in our anchor and getting under weigh, without attracting the Englishman's attention. Expecting a shot at our heels every moment, we sat breathlessly measuring our distance from the brig. Fortunately, we escaped notice, and reached Salem in safety.

Shortly after this adventure, the good citizens of Salem were thrown into a high state of excitement by the noise of a heavy cannonading. A general rush took place from all quarters towards the Neck. I followed with the rest. We found it to be occasioned by the engagement between the *Chesapeake* and *Shannon,* in compliance with a challenge, sent by the latter, which was accepted by Captain Lawrence, of the former. The result is well known. After a short action, the *Chesapeake* struck to the *Shannon,* and was carried away by the victors, in triumph, to Halifax. One reason for the defeat of the American frigate, may perhaps be found in the fact that her crew were newly shipped; some of them were volunteer landsmen, while none of them had what sailors call their sea-legs on. No ship is fit for action until she has been at sea at least a month. In this action the captain, first lieutenant, and several men, were killed. Mr. George Crowninshield sent a vessel to Halifax for the bodies of those gallant officers; they were interred in Salem with naval honors.

My cousin, having now reached home, was desirous to have me devote myself to some business. He proposed that of a sailmaker; but by this time I had quite a desire to go to sea again.

The *Constitution,* the *Frolic* sloop of war, and the gun brig *Siren,* were all shipping hands in Boston. My feelings inclined me towards old *Ironsides;* but my cousin, having sailed with Captain Parker,[1] of the *Siren,* recommended that officer so strongly, that I was induced to join his ship, in company with the quartermaster and several of the former hands of the *United States.* My cousin also overruled my design of shipping in a false name; so that, in defiance of my fears, I suffered myself to be entered as Samuel Leech, on the books of the U. S. brig *Siren,* of sixteen guns. The payment of three months' advance, with the sum I brought with me from New York, enabled me honorably to discharge my board bills at my cousin's, and to purchase a little clothing necessary to fit me for sea. I was then in the seventeenth year of my life.

Once more in a man of war, my seriousness all vanished like mist before the sun. Alas, it was poor soil to nourish the seed of

---

[1] George Parker, formerly first lieutenant of the *Constitution.*

life—barren of everything that related to purity, religion, and immortality.

My first impressions of the American service were very favorable. The treatment in the *Siren* was more lenient and favorable
than in the *Macedonian*. The captain and officers were kind, while
there was a total exemption from that petty tyranny exercised by
the upstart midshipmen in the British service. As a necessary effect, our crew were as comfortable and as happy as men ever are in
a man of war.

While we lay in Boston harbor, Thanksgiving Day arrived.
Some of our Salem men inquired if I was not going home to keep
Thanksgiving, for they all supposed I belonged to Salem. What
they meant by Thanksgiving, was a mystery to me, but, dissem-
bling my ignorance, I obtained leave, determined to learn what it
meant. The result of my visit was the idea that Thanksgiving was
one in which the people crammed themselves with turkeys, geese,
pumpkin-pies, etc.; for, certainly, that was the chief business of
the day, so far as I could perceive. With too many people, I believe
that this is the leading idea associated with the day even now.

Our brig had before this taken in her guns, consisting of two
long nine-pounders, twelve twenty-four pound carronades, and
two forty-two pounders. Our crew was composed of some one
hundred and twenty-five smart, active men. We were all supplied
with stout leather caps, something like those used by firemen.
These were crossed by two strips of iron, covered with bearskin,
and were designed to defend the head, in boarding an enemy's
ship, from the stroke of the cutlass. Strips of bearskin were likewise used to fasten them on, serving the purpose of false whiskers,
and causing us to look as fierce as hungry wolves. We were also
frequently exercised in the various evolutions of a sea-fight; first
using our cannon, then seizing our cutlasses and boarding-spikes,
and cutting to the right and left, as if in the act of boarding an enemy's ship. Thus we spent our time from early in the fall until after
Christmas, when we received orders to hold ourselves in readiness
for sea.

CHAPTER NINE

AS we lay waiting for our final orders, a report reached us that a large English brig of war, called the *Nimrod,* lay in a cove somewhere near Boston bay. Upon this information, our officers planned a night expedition for the purpose of effecting her capture. Our intended mode of attack was to run close alongside, pour a broadside upon her, and then, without further ceremony, board her, cutlass in hand. So we took in our powder, ground up our cutlasses, and towards night got under weigh. A change in the wind, however, defeated our designs, and we put into Salem harbor, with no other result than the freezing of a man's fingers, which happened while we were furling our sails. Thus ended our first warlike expedition in the *Siren.*

Shortly after this affair, we received orders to start on a cruise to the coast of Africa, and, in company with the *Grand Turk*[1] a privateer, set sail from Salem. Passing the fort, we received the usual hail from the sentry, of "Brig ahoy! where are you bound to?"

To this salutation the first lieutenant jocosely answered, "There, and back again, on a man of war's cruise." Such a reply would not have satisfied a British soldier; but we shot past the fort unmolested. After two days we parted company with the *Grand Turk,* and by the aid of a fair wind soon found ourselves in the

---

[1] The *Grand Turk* was a noted privateer, commanded at that time by either Captain Breed or Captain Green, and owned by the famous Salem merchant, William Gray.

Gulf Stream; where, instead of fearing frozen fingers, we could go barefooted and feel quite comfortable.

We now kept a sharp look-out at the mast-head, but met with nothing until we reached the Canary Islands, near which we saw a boat-load of Portuguese, who, coming alongside, talked in their native tongue with great noise and earnestness, but were no more intelligible to us than so many blackbirds.

While off the African coast, our captain died. His wasted body was placed in a coffin, with shot to sink it. After the service had been read, the plank on which the coffin rested was elevated, and it slipped into the great deep. The yards were braced round, and we were under weigh again, when, to our surprise and grief, we saw the coffin floating on the waves. The reason was, the carpenter had bored holes in the top and bottom; he should have made them only in the top.

After the funeral, the crew were called aft, and the first lieutenant, Mr. Nicholson,[1] told us that it should be left to our decision whether he should assume the command and continue the cruise, or return home. We gave him three hearty cheers, in token of our wish to continue the cruise. He was a noble-minded man, very kind and civil to his crew; and the opposite, in every respect, to the haughty, lordly captain with whom I first sailed in the *Macedonian*. Seeing me one day with rather a poor hat on, he called me aft and presented me with one of his own, but little worn. "Good luck to him," said I, in sailor phrase, as I returned to my messmates; "he has a soul to be saved." We also lost two of our crew, who fell victims to the heat of the climate.

One morning the cry of "Sail ho!" directed our attention to a strange sail, which had hove to, with her courses hauled up. At first, we took her for a British man-of-war brig. The hands were summoned to quarters, and the ship got ready for action. A nearer approach, however, convinced us that the supposed enemy, was no other than our old friend, the *Grand Turk*. She did not appear to know us; for no sooner did she see that our craft was a brig of war, than, supposing us to belong to Johnny Bull, she crowded all her canvas, and made the best of her way off. Knowing what she was, we permitted her to escape without further alarm.

The first land we made was Cape Mount. The natives came off to a considerable distance in their canoes, clothed in nothing but a piece of cloth fastened round the waist, and extending downward

---

[1] James B. Nicholson, the same who was on the *United States*.

to the feet. As we approached the shore, we saw several fires burning; this, we were told, in the broken English spoken by our sable visitors, was the signal for trade. We bought a quantity of oranges, limes, coconuts, tamarinds, plantains, yams and bananas. We likewise took in a quantity of cassava, a species of ground root, of which we made tolerable pudding and bread; also a few hogs and some water.

We lay here several days looking out for any English vessels that might come thither for purposes of trade.

Meanwhile, we began to experience the inconvenience of a hot climate. Our men were all covered with blotches or boils, probably occasioned by so sudden a transition from extreme cold to extreme heat. What was worse than this, was the want of a plentiful supply of water. In the absence of this, we were placed on an allowance of two quarts per diem, to each man. This occasioned us much suffering; for, after mixing our Indian for puddings, our cassava for bread, and our whisky for grog, we had but little left to assuage our burning thirst. Some, in their distress, drank large quantities of sea water, which only increased their thirst and made them sick; others sought relief in chewing lead, tea-leaves, or anything which would create moisture. Never did we feel more delighted than when our boat's crew announced the discovery of a pool of fine clear water. We received it with greater satisfaction than ever prodigal did tidings of the death of some rich old relative, to whose well-laden purse he was undisputed heir. We could have joined in the most enthusiastic cold-water song ever sung by either hermit or Washingtonian.[1]

While cruising along the coast, we one night perceived a large ship lying at anchor near the shore. We could not decide whether she was a large merchantman or a man of war; so we approached her with the utmost caution. Our doubts were soon removed, for she suddenly loosed all her sails and made chase after us. By the help of their glasses, our officers ascertained her to be an English frigate. Of course, it was folly to engage her; so we made all the sail we could carry, beat to quarters, lighted our matches, and lay down at our guns, expecting to be prisoners of war before morning. During the night we hung out false lights, and altered our course; this baffled our pursuer; in the morning she was no more to be seen.

The next sail we made was not so formidable. She was an Eng-

---

[1] The Washingtonian was a temperance society of the day.

lish vessel at anchor in the Senegal river. We approached her and hailed. Her officer returned an insolent reply, which so exasperated our captain that he passed the word to fire into her, but recalled it almost immediately. The countermand was too late; for in a moment, everything being ready for action, we poured a whole broadside into our unfortunate foe. The current carried us away from the stranger. We attempted to beat up again, but our guns had roused the garrison in a fort which commanded the river; they began to blaze away at us in so expressive a manner, that we found it prudent to get a little beyond the reach of their shot, and patiently wait for daylight.

The next morning we saw our enemy hauled close in shore, under the protection of the fort, and filled with soldiers. At first, it was resolved to man the boats and cut her out; but this, after weighing the subject maturely, was pronounced to be too hazardous an experiment, and, notwithstanding our men begged to make the attempt, it was wisely abandoned. How many were killed by our hasty broadside, we never learned, but doubtless several poor fellows were hurried to a watery and unexpected grave, affording another illustration of the *beauty* of war. This affair our men humorously styled "the battle of Senegal."

After visiting Cape Three Points, we shaped our course for St. Thomas. On our way, we lost a prize through a display of Yankee cunning in her commander. We had hoisted English colors; the officer in command of the stranger was pretty well versed in the secrets of false colors, and in return he ran up the American flag. The bait took: supposing her to be American, we showed the stars and stripes. This was all the merchantman desired. It told him what we were, and he made all possible sail for St. Thomas. We followed, crowding every stitch of canvas our brig could carry; we also got out our sweeps and swept her along, but in vain. The merchantman was the better sailer, and succeeded in reaching St. Thomas, which, being a neutral port, secured her safety. Her name was the *Jane,* of Liverpool. The next morning, another Liverpool merchantman got into the harbor, unseen by our look-out until she was under the protection of the laws of neutrality.

Our next business was to watch the mouth of the harbor, in the hope of catching them as they left port. But they were too cautious to run into danger, especially as they were expecting a convoy for their protection, which might make us glad to trust more to our canvas than to our cannon.

Shortly after this occurrence, we made another sail standing in towards St. Thomas. Hoisting English colors, our officers also donning the British uniform, we soon came near enough to hail her; for, not doubting that we were a British brig, the merchant-man made no effort to escape us. Our captain hailed her, "Ship ahoy!"

"Halloa!"

"What ship is that?"

"The ship *Barton.*"

"Where do you belong?"

"To Liverpool."

"What is your cargo?"

"Red-wood, palm oil and ivory."

"Where are you bound to?"

"To St. Thomas."

Just at that moment our English flag was hauled down, and, to the inexpressible annoyance of the officers of the *Barton,* the stars and stripes supplied its place.

"Haul down your colors!" continued Captain Nicholson.

The old captain, who, up to this moment, had been enjoying a comfortable nap in his very comfortable cabin, now came upon deck in his shirt sleeves, rubbing his eyes, and looking so exqui-sitely ridiculous, it was scarcely possible to avoid laughing. So surprised was he at the unexpected termination of his dreams, he could not command skill enough to strike his colors; which was accordingly done by the mate. As they had two or three guns aboard, and as some of the men looked as if they would like to fight, our captain told us, if they fired to not "leave enough of her to boil a tin pot with." After this expressive and *classical* threat, we lowered our boats and took possession of this our first prize.

After taking out as much of her cargo as we desired, just at night we set her on fire. It was an imposing sight, to behold the antics of the flames, leaping from rope to rope, and from spar to spar, until she looked like a fiery cloud resting on the dark surface of the water. Presently, her spars began to fall, her masts went by the board, her loaded guns went off, the hull was burned to the water's edge, and what, a few hours before, was a fine, trim ship, looking like a winged creature of the deep, lay a shapeless, charred mass, whose blackened outline, shadowed in the clear, still waves, looked like the grim spirit of war lurking for its prey.

This wanton destruction of property was in accordance with

our instructions, "to *sink, bum* and *destroy*" whatever we took from the enemy. Such is the war-spirit! SiNK, burn and destroy! How it sounds! Yet such are the instructions given by Christian (?) nations to their agents in time of war. What Christian will not pray for the destruction of such a spirit?

The crew of the *Barton* we carried into St. Thomas, and placed them on board the *Jane,* excepting a Portuguese and two colored men, who shipped among our crew. We also took with us a fine black spaniel dog, whom the men called by the name of Paddy. This done, we proceeded to watch for fresh victims, on which to wreak the vengeance of the war-spirit.

The next sail we met, was an English brig, called the *Adventure;* which had a whole menagerie of monkeys on board. We captured and burned her, just as we did the *Barton.* Her crew were also disposed of in the same manner. One of them, an African prince, who had acquired a tolerable education in England, and who was remarkably polite and sensible, shipped in the *Siren.* His name was Samuel Quaqua.

We now remained at St. Thomas several days, carrying on a petty trade with the natives. Our men bought all kinds of fruit, gold dust and birds. For these things, we gave them articles of clothing, tobacco, knives, etc. For an old vest, I obtained a large basket of oranges; for a hand of tobacco, five large coconuts: a profitable exchange on my side; since, although I drew my tobacco of the purser, I fortunately never acquired the habit of using it; a loss I never regretted. My coconuts were far more gratifying and valuable when we got to sea, parched with thirst, and suffering for water, than all the tobacco in the ship.

While in this port, I had to throw myself on the protection of the officers, to avoid the disposition to abuse which existed in one of the petty officers. Several of these gentlemen, who messed together, had a large boy to wait on them. He was unacquainted with naval usages, and somewhat awkward withal. This led them to oppress him: they frequently knocked him round, and even ventured to flog him with a rope's-end. The poor lad used to cry, and fret about it, leading quite a miserable life. By some means, it happened that I was ordered to take his place; and I determined to resist their habit of punishing their servant; so, one day, when the gunner came below for his share of the whisky, and found it was gone, his messmates having drank the whole, and asked me for his whisky, I boldly answered "I know nothing about it."

At this, he broke out into a furious passion, declaring that if I did not find his whisky he would have my heart's blood.

To this *dignified* and *manly* threat I made no reply, but proceeded forthwith to the first lieutenant, and laid the facts before him. The gunner was sent for, reprimanded, and threatened with degradation, if ever he either struck or offered to strike me again. Of course, I had no further trouble with these would-be tyrants.

The only other difficulty I ever had on board the *Siren,* was with a young midshipman, who was on his first voyage—who was, in sailor's language, "a real green-horn." He ordered me, one day, to wash his clothes. I refused, saying it was not my duty. Putting on the air of a pompous man, he told me it was my duty to obey an officer, and I should do it. I persisted in resisting this sprig of American aristocracy, and as I heard no more of it, I suppose he learned that he was in the wrong.

The effect of my conduct on the gunner was seen a short time afterwards, in the following little incident, which will also show the reader the nature of the pranks practiced in men of war, by the hands. The gunner was a very selfish man, and somehow, when we were on short allowance of water, he contrived to keep a keg filled, which he kept in a small state-room; and a man might choke before he would part with a drop. One night, when my throat was parched with thirst, I met the boatswain's mate, and said, "If I were minded to play the rogue, I could hook some water."

The mate, who was as dry as myself, looked mightily gratified at this piece of news, and asked, "Where?"

"I have a key that will fit the lock of the room where the gunner keeps his water keg."

"Well," said he," give me the key. I will be the rogue, while you keep watch for the old gunner."

After drinking all we desired, we locked the door and returned to our posts, wondering how the gunner would feel when he found that some one had been practicing the arithmetical rule, called reduction, on his water keg.

The next day the offended gunner threw out sundry hints to his messmates about his loss, indirectly charging them with the robbery. This drew down their wrath upon him, and he was compelled to be content with swallowing his choler, and getting a new lock for his state-room. In all his rage he never uttered a word to me: he had not forgotten my appeal to his superiors.

From St. Thomas we proceeded to Angola, where we staid long enough to clean, paint and refit our brig, from stem to stern. This was the last port we intended to touch at on the coast of Africa. Our next anchorage was to be in Boston harbor—at least so we purposed; but Providence and the British ordered it otherwise.

To accomplish our object, we had to run the gauntlet through the host of English cruisers that hovered about, like birds of prey, along both sides of the Atlantic coast. This enterprise appeared so impossible to my mind, while we lay at Angola, and the fear of being retaken and hung operated so strongly on my imagination, that, more than once, I determined to run away and find a refuge among the Africans; but my better judgment prevailed at last, and I continued at my post.

Still, I used every possible precaution to escape detection in case of our capture. In accordance with the custom of our navy at that period, I let my hair grow long behind. To change my looks more effectually, instead of tying mine in a cue as the others did, I let it hang in ringlets all round my face and neck. This, together with the effect of time, caused me to appear quite a different lad from what I was, when a boy, on board the *Macedonian*. I also adopted that peculiarity of dress practiced by American men-of-war's-men, which consisted in wearing my shirt open at the neck, with the corners thrown back. On these corners a device was wrought, consisting of the stars of the American flag, with the British flag underneath. By these means I hoped to pass for a genuine Yankee, without suspicion, in case we should fall into English hands.

Having finished our preparations, we left Angola for Boston. We reached the island of Ascension in safety, where was a post-office of a truly patriarchal character. A box is nailed to a post near the shore. Ships that pass send to the box and deposit or take out letters, as the case may be. This is probably the cheapest general post-office establishment in the world.

We had scarcely left this island before the cry of "Sail ho!" arrested every ear. Supposing her to be a large merchantman, we made towards her; but a nearer approach made it doubtful whether she was an Indiaman or a man of war. The captain judged her to be the latter, and tacked ship immediately. He was unwilling to place himself in the situation of an American privateer, who, mistaking a seventy-four for a merchantman, ran his ship close alongside, and boldly summoned her to haul down her colors. The captain of the other ship coolly replied, "I am not in the habit of striking my colors." At the same moment the ports of his ship were opened, and disclosed her long ranges of guns, yawning over the decks of the privateer. Perceiving his mistake, the privateer, with admirable tact and good humor, said, "Well, if you won't, I will," and pulling down his bunting, surrendered to his more powerful foe. To avoid such a mistake as this, our captain made all sail to escape the coming stranger, which was now bearing down upon us under a heavy pressure of canvas, revealing, as she gained upon our little brig, that she bore the formidable character of a seventy-four gun ship, under English colors.

Of course, fighting was out of the question. It would be like the assault of a dog on an elephant, or a dolphin on a whale. We therefore crowded all possible sail, threw our guns, cables, anchors, hatches, etc, overboard, to increase her speed. But it soon became apparent that we could not escape. The wind blew quite fresh, which gave our opponent the advantage: she gained on us very fast. We shifted our course, in hopes to baffle her until night, when we felt pretty sure of getting out of her way. It was of no use, she still gained, until we saw ourselves almost within gun-shot of our opponent.

In this extremity, the captain ordered the quartermaster, George Watson, to throw the private signals overboard. This was a hard task for the bold-hearted fellow. As he pitched them into the sea, he said, "Good-bye, brother Yankee;" an expression which, in spite of their mortifying situation, forced a smile from the lips of the officers.

The sound of a gun now came booming through the air. It was a signal for us to heave to, or to look out for consequences. What might have been, we learned afterwards, for a division of the crew of the seventy-four had orders to sink us if we made the least show of resistance. Finding it useless to prolong the chase, our commander reluctantly ordered the flag to be struck. We then hove to, and our foe came rolling down upon us, looking like a huge avalanche rushing down the mountain side to crush some poor peasant's dwelling. Her officers stood on her quarter deck, glancing unutterable pride, while her captain shouted, "What brig is that? "

"The United States brig *Siren,*" replied Captain Nicholson.

"This is his Britannic Majesty's ship *Medway!*"[1] he answered. "I claim you as my lawful prize."

Boats were then lowered, the little brig taken from us, and our crew transferred to the *Medway,* stowed away in the cable tier,

---

[1] Captain Augustus Bruce (James' *Hist. British Navy).*

and put in messes of twelve, with an allowance of only eight men's rations to a mess; a regulation which caused us considerable suffering from hunger. The sight of the marines on board the *Medway* made me tremble, for my fancy pointed out several of them as having formerly belonged to the *Macedonian*. I realty feared I was destined to speedily swing at the yard-arm; it was, however, a groundless alarm.

This event happened July 12, 1814. Only eight days before, we had celebrated the independence of our country, by dancing and splicing the main-brace. Now we had a fair prospect of a rigorous imprisonment. Such are the changes which constantly occur under the rule of the war-spirit.

The day subsequent to our capture, we were marched to the quarter deck with our clothes-bags, where we underwent a strict search. We were ordered to remove our outside garments for this purpose. They expected to find us in possession of large quantities of gold dust. What little our crew had purchased was taken from them, with a spirit of rapacity altogether beneath the dignity of a naval commander.

Our short allowance was a source of much discomfort in this our prison-ship. But, in the true spirit of sailors, we made even this a subject of coarse jests and pleasant remark. Some would sit and paint the luxuries of shore life until our mouths watered at the idea of soft tack, fried eggs, sausages, and those other delicacies which go to make up a sailor's idea of a sensual paradise. Others would discourse about roast beef, boiled lamb, and caper sauce; to which some old weather-beaten tar would answer, "Give me the lamb and a knife and fork, and I will cut capers enough." This would draw out peals of laughter, to be followed by various yarns of feasts gone by, and of sprees enjoyed on liberty and paydays. Thus we beguiled our time; though, with all our laughing,, we could not laugh away the clamors of our hungry stomachs; and when I took my turn of a few minutes on deck, the gift of a piece of hard, dry biscuit, afforded me more gustatory delight, than would the taste of the richest pound-cake, now that I have an abundance of food.

Enduring this evil, we proceeded on our course. When the *Medway* arrived at Simon's Town, about twenty-one miles from the Cape of Good Hope, we met the *Denmark*, seventy-four, on her way to England, with prisoners from Cape Town. The captain had hitherto intended to land us at the latter place, but the presence of the *Denmark* led him to change his purpose, and land us at Simon's Town.

The journey from this place to the Cape was one of great suffering to our crew. We were received on the beach by a file of Irish soldiers. Under their escort we proceeded seven miles, through heaps of burning sand, seeing nothing worthy of notice on the way, but a number of men busily engaged in cutting up dead whales on the sea-shore.

After resting a short time, we recommenced our march, guarded by a new detachment of soldiers. Unused to walking as we were, we began to grow excessively fatigued; and, after wading a stream of considerable depth, we were so overcome, that it seemed impossible to proceed any farther. We lay down, discouraged and wretched, on the sand. The guard brought us some bread, and gave half-a-pint of wine to each man. This revived us somewhat. We were now placed under a guard of dragoons. They were very kind, and urged us to attempt the remaining seven miles. To relieve us, they carried our clothes-bags on their horses; and overtaking some Dutch farmers, going to the Cape with broom-stuff and brush, the officer of the dragoons made them carry the most weary among us in their wagons. It is not common for men to desire the inside of a prison, but I can assure my readers we did most heartily wish ourselves there, on that tedious journey. At last, about nine o'clock, P.M., we arrived at Cape Town, having left one of our number at Wineburg, through exhaustion, who joined us the next day. Stiff, sore, and weary, we hastily threw ourselves on the hard boards of our prison, where, without needing to be soothed or rocked, we slept profoundly until late the next morning. For a description of our prison, with what happened to us there, the reader is referred to the succeeding chapter.

CHAPTER TEN

THE next morning we took a survey of our new quarters. We found ourselves placed in a large yard, surrounded by high walls, and strongly guarded by soldiers. Within this enclosure, there was a building, or shed, composed of three rooms, neither of which had any floor. Round the sides stood three, benches or stages, one above the other, to serve for berths. On these we spread our hammocks and bed-clothes, making them tolerably comfortable places to sleep in. A few of the men preferred to sling their hammocks, as they did at sea. Here, also, we used to eat, unless, as was our frequent practice, we did so in the open air.

Our officers had been sent thirty miles inland, so that we had lost the natural exactors of discipline among seamen. To remedy this deficiency, our first step was to adopt a set of regulations in respect to order, cleanliness, etc, and to appoint certain of our number to enforce them.

We experienced some unpleasantness, at first, from the insolence of some of the sergeants commanding the prison guard. Most of these petty officers were very friendly and kind, but two or three of them manifested a surly, tyrannical temper, annoying us in many little things, enough to embitter our enjoyment, while they were on duty. This petty despotism we soon cured, by returning their abuse in a rather provoking kind of coin. We used to plague them by causing a long delay when the hour arrived for them to be relieved. They were required to muster us every morning, that we might be counted before the new guard took us in charge. On those occasions some would purposely absent themselves; others were sent to find the absentees; these, in their turn, would hide themselves, and require to be sought by others. This was excessively vexatious to the soldiers, and as it occurred only when a tyrannical sergeant was on guard, they soon understood its meaning. The plan was successful, and we thus got rid of one source of discomfort.

Our next difficulty was with the old Dutchman, named Badiem, who furnished our prison with provisions. He had already learned the difficulty of cheating a Yankee; for the Americans who were carried away in the *Denmark* had been in this same prison, and had taught the old man that they were rougher customers than the Frenchmen who had preceded them. We gave him another lesson.

He undertook to wrong us and benefit himself by furnishing a very inferior article of bread. After counseling among ourselves, we took the following plan to bring him to his senses:

We were visited every day by a superior officer, called the officer of the day. He was a kind old man, who had seen service in the war of the revolution, and was at the battle of Bunker Hill. He had a profound respect for the American character, and could not speak of that great action without tears. One day a friendly sergeant being on duty, we gave him a piece of the old Dutchman's bread, complaining bitterly of its quality. When the old officer came round as usual, on a fine, dashing charger, and asked his customary question of "All right?" our friend the sergeant replied, "No, sir!"

"What is the matter?" asked the venerable old gentleman.

"The prisoners complain of their bread, sir," said the sergeant.

"Let me see it," answered the general. The sergeant gave him a small piece. He examined it, wrapped it up carefully in some paper, clapped the spurs to his horse, and rode off. The next day, we had better bread than ever before, and an order came for a man from each room to go with the sentry to the town every morning, to examine our daily provision; and, if not what it should be, to reject it. This completely upset the golden visions of the old Dutchman.

With much choler he exclaimed, "I had rather have one thousand Frenchmen, than one hundred Yankees."

We could not now complain of our fare. We had an abundance of beef and mutton, beside a full allowance of bread, etc. The beef, to be sure, was poor, lean stuff, but the mutton was excellent. The sheep at the Cape have a peculiarity, which may cause the reader to smile. They have enormously large, flat tails, weighing from twelve to twenty pounds. These are regularly sold by the pound for purposes of cookery. Should any one treat this statement as a forecastle yarn, I refer him to the descriptions of these sheep, given by travelers and naturalists.[1]

Besides our prison allowance, we had opportunity to purchase as many little luxuries and niceties as our slender finances would permit. These were furnished by a slave, who was the property of the old Dutchman, and who was so far a favorite as to be indulged with two wives, and the privilege of selling sundry small articles to the prisoners. This sable polygamist furnished us with coffee, made from burnt barley, for a *doublegee* (an English penny)[2] per pint; the same sum would purchase a sausage, a piece of fish, or a glass of rum. On equally reasonable terms, he furnished us with blackberries, oranges, etc. Our men, who, by the way had eaten fruit in every quarter of the globe, and were therefore competent judges, pronounced the latter the best in the world. The berries afforded me a rich treat at Christmas.

To obtain means for the purchase of these dainties, our men braided hats, wrought at mechanical employments, or at such pursuits as their respective tastes and capacities suggested. These occupations served to beguile our confinement of much of its tediousness.

Still, we had many vacant, listless hours. To fill them, we resorted to the demoralizing practice of gambling. A game with balls, called shake-bag, loo, venture, all-fours, etc. occupied our evening hours, and sometimes the whole night. It was not uncommon for

---

[1] The Barbary sheep entirely resembles the tame kind, excepting in the tail, which is very much loaded with fat, is often more than a foot broad, and weighs upwards of twenty pounds. Among this kind of broad-tailed sheep, there are some whose tails are so long and heavy, that the shepherds are obliged to fasten a small board with wheels, to support them as they walk along. This tail, which is a substance between marrow and fat, is considered a great delicacy.—*See System of Natural History. Boston: Carter, Hendee & Co., 1834.*

[2] Twenty-four doublegees made a rix dollar. [Expansion] A "rix dollar" is a semi-slang English term which refers to almost any northern European coin (German: Reichsthaler, Dutch: Rijksdaalder, Danish: Rigsdaler, Swedish: Riksdaler). It was also applied to the currency of the Cape Colony. [Fireship Press Editor]

the game to be protracted beyond the midnight hour of Saturday, into the sacred moments of the holy Sabbath. On one of these guilty mornings, some of us, on retiring to a shed, found the dead body of a black slave, hanging by the rope, with which, in a moment of unpardonable despair, he had committed the horrid crime of suicide. The hour, the scene, the place, our recent guilty profanation of God's holy day, conspired to fill many of us with profound dread. In my own mind it led to a few transient purposes of amendment. Alas! When the bright sun arose, these purposes had vanished. The influence of vice triumphed. I grew more and more hardened in wickedness.

Cape Town contained a large slave population. These poor wretches had been extremely degraded under the rule of the Dutch. It was said that their condition had been essentially improved since the conquest of the place by the English. Still, as the suicide just mentioned demonstrated, slavery was a bitter draught. The British have done wisely since then in granting freedom to the slaves in all their colonies. May the whole world imitate the noble example!

We were subjected to frequent and violent gales of wind while here. The approach of these storms was always faithfully proclaimed by the mountain that towered up behind us; a large white cloud, resting on its summit, like a tablecloth, was a certain indication of the elemental warfare. Whenever this phenomenon appeared, our men used to remark, "Look out for a blow, the cloth is beginning to spread." Very soon the vessels in the bay could be seen striking their top-gallant masts and yards, and sometimes even housing their top-masts. In a few minutes the ocean would give signs of the coming commotion; the waves became crested with clouds of foam, and the spirit of the storm was seen careering in triumph over the liquid mountains of the angry deep.

Besides Table mountain, there was another near it, called the Lion's Rump, from its similarity to that noble animal in a sitting posture. On the summit of this mountain was a telegraph, which informed us, in common with the people of the Cape, of the approach of shipping to the harbor.

At the town, the British had a hospital for the accommodation of their army and navy. The advantages of this institution were humanely and properly offered to us, whenever we were sick. Happening to be quite unwell one day, my shipmates advised me to go thither. Now, on board the *Siren,* when in a similar state, the surgeon had administered an ounce of Glauber salts. The dose caused such nausea, that from that time I held salts in profound abhorrence. When the hospital was suggested to me, I associated it with the idea of salts, and, shuddering, remarked that "I would go if I thought they would not give me salts." My shipmates all said they thought I should not have salts prescribed: so, under the guard of a sentry, I sallied forth to the hospital. "Well, my boy," said the doctor, "what's the matter with you?"

With many wry faces, I told him my symptoms; when, to my inconceivable mortification and disgust, he spoke to a sort of lob-lolly boy, who waited upon him, and said, "Doctor Jack! Bring this boy six ounces of salts."

This was intolerable. One ounce had sickened me for months at the bare mention of salts, and now I was to swallow six! It seemed impossible. The remedy was worse than the disease. I wished myself back at my quarters. This was, however, in vain, unless I took a dangerous leap from the window. I must submit. The salts were brought, but they were not so bad, either in quality or quantity, as my dose in the *Siren*. The reason I found to consist in the fact, that they were Epsom instead of Glauber, and that the six ounces included the weight of the water in which they were dissolved. So well was I pleased with my visit to the hospital, and especially with the privilege afforded me of walking about the streets of Cape Town, that I afterwards feigned illness to gain another admission. I was willing to take the salts for the sake of the liberty of jaunting about the streets. Of the sin of lying I thought nothing. I was a sailor, caring little for aught but present gratification. The beauty of truth I had never seen; the hatefulness of a lie I had never learned. Most gratefully do I acknowledge that Divine goodness, which has since effectually taught me both the one and the other.

At Cape Town there was a small prison, called the "Trunk." To this place those of our number, who were disorderly, were sent, to be closely confined, on no other diet than bread and water, for as many days as the commandant might designate. We always quietly permitted any offender among us to be sent thither without resistance: but when, on one occasion, an attempt was made to confine two of our shipmates unjustly, we gave them a demonstration, which saved us afterwards from any similar attempt.

Two of our men had hung out some clothes, they had just washed, in our yard, near their own shed. Now, it happened that the doctor to the military stationed at the Cape, had an entrance to his office through our yard. The clothes were undesignedly hung across his path, compelling him either to stoop a little in passing, or to ask their removal. He was too proud to adopt either of these peaceful methods, but, with manifest spitefulness, he took out his knife and cut the line, so that the clothes fell into the dirt. The owners, seeing their wet clothing in this condition, broke out into passionate inquiries after the offender. "It was the English doctor," replied one of our shipmates, who had witnessed the whole affair. This brought forth a volley of sailors' oaths from the offended parties. The enraged doctor overheard their wrathful ebullitions, and, without further ceremony, ordered the two men to be carried to the "Trunk."

Here, then, was a manifest case of injustice. We resolved not to submit to it, let the consequences be what they might. When the sergeant came in for the doctor's victims, we all turned out in a body, declaring we would all go to the "Trunk" together. The sergeant, seeing us in this state of rebellion, called out the whole guard, and ordered them to load and fire upon us. We were not however so easily scared. We shouted, "Fire away! You will have but one fire, and then it will be our turn." At the same time we picked up all the broken glass, sticks, stones, etc, which were within our reach, and stood waiting for their firing as the signal for a general *melee*. The sergeant, seeing our resolution, and wisely considering that our superiority in numbers, might secure us a victory over the handful composing his guard, ordered the soldiers to retire. We never heard any more of the little doctor's indignation: it probably evaporated, like the moisture from the clothes his petty indignation had thrown to the ground. How insignificant such acts appear, in men professing to be gentlemen!

Shortly after this event, we were thrown into confusion and temporary excitement, by the approach of a large party to our prison, at midnight, attended by a band of music. We turned out and rushed to the gate of our yard. The guard turned out likewise, trembling under the impression that our countrymen had captured the town and were coming to give us our liberty. Their fears and our wonder were quieted, however, by a speedy discovery of the true character of this midnight party. It was a Dutch wedding, coming to the house of the old Dutchman, our caterer; the entrance to which being in our yard, the party had to pass directly through our territories; which they did, their band playing the tune of ' A free and accepted Mason."

Notwithstanding we were in tolerably comfortable circumstances, our confinement soon became exceedingly irksome. We pined for freedom; we longed to get once more where the "old gridiron" floated in fearless triumph. A report of the burning of Washington by the British added not a little to our desire. We began to talk of home. This led to other suggestions; these to the formation of plans for our escape. We at length concerted a measure, which was, to break from the prison in the night, disarm and confine the guard, help ourselves to boats, and cut out some large ship, in which we might make our escape to America. The success of this plot, however, was never tested; for, reaching the ears of the commander, the guards were strengthened; the light dragoons ordered out to patrol the harbor; and such other preventive measures adopted, as cut off all hope of forcible escape. Our only remedy for this disappointment, was submission, and boasting of what we would have done, had we got into the strife for liberty.

As the period of our imprisonment drew towards a close, we were informed that the Rev. George Thorn, a missionary, was desirous to come and preach to us. Some of our men objected, because, they said, he would preach about his king, and they had no desire to hear anything about kings. Others said, "Let him come; we will hear him with attention, and if we don't like him we can afterwards stay away. At any rate, don't let us abuse him; but rather show him that Americans know what is good behavior."

This reply shows the true spirit of the mass of seamen in respect to religion; for though they care little about personal piety, they will not, usually, unless intoxicated, insult a minister. This was once shown in the experience of the eccentric Rowland Hill; when a mob threatened the old gentleman with mischief, some sailors present rallied round him, threatening vengeance on any who dared to insult the preacher.

Accordingly, we sent our respects to Mr. Thorn, inviting him to favor us with a visit. We then cleaned and fitted up one room with benches. The following Sabbath he came. His preaching was earnest, simple and interesting. Instead of discoursing about kings, as some had predicted, the only king about whom he preached, was the King of heaven. We invited him to come again. He accepted the invitation, and our meetings soon began to be profitable and interesting. We had singing, for several of our men were tolerable singers, and they were aided by the presence of some pious soldiers from the garrison, and occasionally by Mrs. Thorn, the amiable lady of our excellent preacher. Our officers, too, frequently came from their residence, and were pleased to see the good order and happiness apparent on these occasions. I assure my readers, that the most delightful moments of our imprisonment were those we spent in singing some sweet hymn, in the good old-fashioned tunes of *Bridgewater, Russia, Wells, etc.*

Among the texts used by Mr. Thorn, I remember the following: "Turn ye to the strong-hold, ye prisoners of hope;" Zech. ix. 12. "Behold, I stand at the door and knock," etc; Rev. iii. 20. "And yet there is room;" Luke xiv. 22. It was realty pleasing to hear the various remarks made by our men, after listening to faithful discourses from these and similar texts. One would remark, "He hit me a clew." To this another would reply, "He shot away my colors." A third would add, "He shot away my rigging;" while a fourth would say, "He gave me a shot;" and a fifth, "He gave me a broadside." Thus, in their rough way, did they express the impressions made on their minds by the discourse.

Mr. Thorn was a faithful servant of his Master, the Lord Jesus Christ. He did not rest satisfied with these public efforts, but, during the week, he visited us for the purpose of serious conversation. Several of us were really under strong conviction, and would confess, at these inquiry meetings, and to each other as we paced the yard, how often we had sinned, even cursing our Maker when on the yard at night, amid the roaring of the storm, the bellowing of the thunder, and the angry flashing of the lightning. A happy practical effect followed. Gambling ceased, cards and shake-bag lost their charms. The time was spent in reading useful books. Bibles and religious books were given or loaned to us. Among these were Baxter's *Call,* Doddridge's *Rise and Progress of Religion, etc.* To some extent we were altered men. Had we remained much longer under these gracious influences, most of us, I think, would have become experimental Christians. As it was, the seed was not wholly wasted. Impressions were made, which, no doubt, have, in many cases, yielded rich fruit long before this.

My own mind was strongly wrought upon. A singular dream added to my seriousness. In my dream, I saw myself drowning, while a fierce-looking soldier was pointing his loaded musket at my head. Thus death threatened me from two sources. In this extremity my anguish was very great. All *my* gracious opportunities passed before me, but now it seemed too late for salvation. "Oh," thought I in my sleep, "what would I give, if this were only a dream! How faithfully would I serve the Lord when I awoke." Just at that moment I did awake, scarcely able to convince myself that the ideal scene was not an awful reality. That day I eagerly sought the missionary, and sat with serious delight listening to his instructions. Still I did not give myself up to the service of Christ. So difficult was it for me to make the requisite sacrifice of my beloved sins.

Just at this interesting crisis, a glad report of peace between England and America reached our prison. With joyful faces we assembled round the good man, when he came that day, to inquire if it was really so. While he assured us of its truth, he mildly asked "if it was peace with Heaven;" assuring us that it was a matter of the greatest importance for us to be at peace with God.

As a memento of our esteem for Mr. Thom, we made him several little presents. One of them was a hat made from a bullock's horn. The horn was peeled into narrow slips, these were scraped, split, and braided like straw, and then sewed together. We also made him a model of a ship, fully rigged from stem to stern. The missionary received these marks of our regard with evident pleasure; and, no doubt, when looking upon them afterwards, offered many a prayer for the salvation of the prisoners, who were, for many weeks, the subjects of his anxiety and labors. Blessings rest on him, if he yet lives! Peace to his ashes, if he slumbers among the dead!

Great was the joy of my companions, when the news reached us that we were to embark shortly, in the *Cumberland,* seventy-four, for England. Little was now said or done, except what related to our departure. With strange, yet common perversity of conduct, serious matters were laid aside for the one absorbing thought, "W e shall soon be free!" Thus, an event which should have given birth to gratitude and religious service, only served for an occasion of further neglect and unthankfulness. How strangely wicked is the human heart!

For myself, the tidings filled me with fear. Directly to America I would have gladly gone; but to be carried to England, in one of her ships of war, was like going to certain death. How was it possible for me to escape detection? How could I avoid meeting with some old *Macedonians,* who would, of course, recognize and betray me? These questions had resolved me to volunteer to remain at the Cape, a short time before, when some of our number were sent to England. Now, they tortured me beyond endurance. I felt like an escaped criminal with the officers of justice at his heels. Death at the yard-arm haunted me day and night, like the fancied ghost of a murdered man, staring ghastly at the window of his murderer. No one can imagine my uneasiness, unless he has been placed in a similar situation. I made many promises to God that if he would carry me in safety to America, I would cease to be a swearer, and would most punctually attend his house every Sabbath. These things constituted my highest ideas of human duty at that time; but even these promises, like those made during the heat of the battle in the *Macedonian,* were made to be broken.

After a little delay, we were conveyed on board the *Cumberland,* where we soon heard the well-known summons of "All hands up anchor, ahoy!" A cloud of canvas dropped from her gigantic yards; the sportive breeze came obedient to our wish; and the huge form of the *Cumberland,* accompanied by a large convoy of merchant vessels, was borne rapidly along upon the yielding waves. Cape Town, Table Mountain, the Lion's Rump, and our prison-yard, were soon left far behind, leaving no traces of their existence on the distant horizon; they were to be known to us hereafter only among the images of the brain—as recollections, not as realities. We had spent eight months in the prison of Cape Town.

Our treatment in this ship was superior to what we received in the *Medway.* Instead of the cable tier, we had berths on the upper gun deck, and our allowance of food was sufficient for our wants.

Arriving at St. Helena, we remained a few days in port. This rough, rock-bound island had not yet received its future prisoner, the emperor of France. Here we were removed from the *Cumberland.* Twenty-four of us were sent on board the *Grampus,* of fifty guns, the rest were sent home in our old conqueror, the *Medway;* my lot being cast among the former.

This transfer to the *Grampus* greatly alarmed me; since the more men I saw, the greater, of course, was my chance of detection. I had already escaped being known on board of two seventy-fours; but I could not promise myself the same impunity much longer. However, as I saw no one whose face was familiar, when I went on board, I felt a little more easy. But that night, I had occasion for great trepidation and alarm. About nine o'clock, I heard the order from an officer, of "Pass the word for the boy Leech." This was followed by several voices hallooing, "Boy Leech! Boy Leech!" My heart beat like a triphammer against my bosom, and a cold sweat crept over my whole body. My shipmates said they meant me; but I would not reply. After a few moments, I breathed more freely, and the fear of death passed away. I heard some one saying, "Your master wants you;" which convinced me that there was a "Boy Leech" among the crew of the *Grampus,* as well as another boy Leech among the American prisoners.

On our passage, we made a strange sail. Coming up to her, to our infinite satisfaction we beheld the stars and stripes at her mast-head. "Brother Jonathan has come to town," said one of our men. "He is a most welcome visitor," the rest replied; for indeed "the old gridiron" never looked so pleasant as it did then. This meeting confirmed us in the report of peace between the two nations. This was as gratifying to the crew of the *Grampus* as to us; for they had recently heard that the war with France was ended, and they were all hoping to get discharged. This expectation was defeated, however, by intelligence from some passing ship, that Napoleon was at Paris again, with a force of sixty thousand men.

Nothing could exceed the joy of the officers, and the vexation of the crew, at this piece of information. The former dreaded a peace, because it would place many of them on half-pay; while the chances of war inspired them with hopes of promotion; hence they ran alongside almost every ship in the fleet, shouting, "Have you heard the news? Bonaparte has got to Paris with sixty thousand men!" Really, some of them seemed crazy with joy at the idea of protracted war. Not so, however, the seamen; they longed for peace, since war only brought them hard usage, wounds and death.

While, therefore, the officers were rejoicing, they were muttering curses and oaths, wishing Bonaparte and his army at perdition. Nor was it strange that they felt thus; for the discipline on board the *Grampus* was excessively severe. They were constantly flogging in the most harsh and cruel maimer. The *Sirens* were astonished at what they saw; for on board our brig, we seldom saw more than a dozen lashes inflicted at one time, and that not very often.

At last we came in sight of the white cliffs of old England. To avoid suspicion, I appeared much interested in everything I saw on the coast, and asked the men all those questions which are natural to a stranger, when he sees a new country for the first time. These inquiries they answered with the utmost good humor; for an Englishman is proud of his country, notwithstanding he may find hard usage from her hands.

My American friends have frequently asked if my language did not excite suspicion that I was English. It never did to my knowledge; indeed, so free was I from English provincialisms, that it was often remarked to me, that I "needed no protection;" meaning, that I should be taken for a Yankee, without offering proof.

With all this in my favor, I could not behold myself approaching my native soil, without many misgivings. To a man who knows a halter is hanging over his head, everything furnishes cause for alarm; a piercing look, a whisper, or the sudden mention of his name, is a cause of disquietude, sufficient to stir his inmost soul. Captain Nicholson gave me no little uneasiness, by sending for me one day, just before we arrived in port, to make some inquiries about Mr. Crowninshield, of Salem, Mass. Luckily, I could say I had seen him; beyond that, I could give no further information. He supposed me to be a native of Salem, while I was quaking, through a fearful expectation of being found nearly as ignorant of that city, as I had been, on another occasion, of the city of Philadelphia.

At length we reached Spithead, and were removed to an old prison-ship, called the *Puissant,* which had once belonged to the French. Here we were treated with great lenity; we were even allowed liberty to go on shore. Had I dared, I would have run away; the dread of the halter restrained me! I did not even venture to write, lest my mother should be tempted to visit me, or even to write; since even a letter from any place in England, might awaken suspicion concerning my true character.[1]

After a stay of several weeks in the old *Puissant,* orders came for our transfer to the *Rover,* a gun-brig, which had orders to carry us to Plymouth. Here was a double risk again before me. I had to risk being known by the crew of the *Rover,* and by the many persons who had known me at Plymouth. However, the good hand of Providence was with me to preserve me. We reached our port in safety, where, to our great delight, we heard that the *Woodrop Simms,* of Philadelphia, was to be the Cartel to convey us to America.

Before we were allowed to tread her decks, however, we had to spend two or three days on board the *Royal Sovereign,* of one

---

[1] An instance of maternal imprudence was said to have occurred in this port on board another ship. A poor woman went on board and inquired for her son, who had run from the British service, and was then among the captive crew of an American prize. They told her there was no one of that name among the crew. "He is among the Yankees," said she. Hearing this, the prisoners were called up, and the poor, affectionate, but ill-judging mother, singled out her son, and embracing him, said, "I have brought you a clean shirt! "

The lieutenant, who stood by them, stepped up, remarking to the thunder-stricken man, "It's a clean shirt you want, is it? I will give you a clean handkerchief"—meaning that he would be hung. The unhappy youth was accordingly ironed, in presence of the astounded mother, who now beheld herself the unintentional murderess of her son. A court-martial was held, and the brutal prediction of the lieutenant verified.

hundred and ten guns, because the *Woodrop Simms* was not quite ready to receive us. Here I was exposed to the gaze of eight hundred men; but none of them knew me. Indeed, this was my most hazardous situation; for the *Sovereign* and *Macedonian* had sailed in company before the capture of the latter. Whenever any of her men came near our quarters, I endeavored to look cross-eyed, or closed one eye so as to appear partially blind; and in various other ways altered my appearance, so that even an old shipmate would have been puzzled to recognize me at first.

At last, the grateful news reached us that the Cartel was ready. We went on board with great gaiety, where we met our shipmates who had left the Cape before us. They had been confined in the celebrated Dartmoor prison, with a number of other prisoners, where they had met with rather rough treatment and rougher fare. They were present at what they called the Massacre. Several of the prisoners were detected in an effort to escape. To strike terror into the poor victims, Captain Shortland ordered his men to fire in upon them. Quite a number were killed, and more wounded, by this cold-blooded act; the rest sought the shelter of the prison walls. Several Americans suffered in this wanton assault. Our meeting at this juncture was a source of mutual gratulation.

Our ship was now surrounded with boats containing provisions of all descriptions. To our surprise, the Dartmoor men bought freely of everything. Where they obtained their money, we could not imagine. We learned afterwards that their stock consisted of counterfeit coins, manufactured by the prisoners! It was well for them that our ship put to sea before John Bull's peace officers received information of the fraud. What a school for every species of vice is opened by war! The corruptions and vices occasioned by the operation of this system, are beyond the power of the imagination to conceive.

My feelings were peculiar as I beheld my native land receding from my vision. I was happy, and yet sad. Happy, because I was now safe; sad, because I was again leaving the soil which held my mother and my friends. On the whole, my joyous feelings prevailed.

A few days out, we were hailed by an English frigate. She sent a boat alongside to make some inquiries, and left us to pursue our way in peace. We were all in good spirits; our men being divided into watches to assist the crew of the ship; our officers all snugly quartered in the cabin, and myself appointed to assist the steward; an office quite agreeable to one who had lived on prisoners' fare more than a year,[1] because it brought me a few of the spare luxuries from the officers' table.

One morning, shortly after the English frigate had boarded us, Captain Nicholson asked me something about Salem. I smiled. He inquired why I laughed. "Sir," said I, "Salem is not my native place by considerable."

"What do you mean?" asked the captain, looking somewhat puzzled at my manner of treating the subject.

I then unfolded the secret of my having been one of the crew captured in the *Macedonian.* They seemed amazed at the risks I had encountered since the capture of the *Siren,* and congratulated me very warmly on my really hair-breadth escape from the halter. It was a fortunate escape indeed, for which I can never be sufficiently thankful to that All-seeing Eye, that watched for my safety in the moment of peril.

During this voyage, a great deal was said about quitting the seas and settling down in quietness ashore. One of our shipmates, named William Carpenter, who belonged to Rhode Island, had a particular enthusiasm in favor of farming. He promised to take me with him, where I could learn the art of cultivating the soil. Many of us made strong resolutions to embark in some such enterprise. The pleasures of agriculture were sung and praised among us in so ardent a manner, that he must have been incredulous indeed, who could have doubted, for a moment, the certainty of quite a number of our hands becoming farmers, whenever we should gain the land.

One night we lay in our hammocks, talking with great earnestness about our favorite scheme, the wind blowing quite freshly on deck. Said one, "If I ever get home, you won't catch me on board of a ship again." "Yes," said another; "farmers live well, at any rate. They are not put on allowance, but have enough to eat: if they work hard all day, they can turn in at night; and if it blows hard, the house won't rock much, and there's no sails to reef." While this and similar conversation was going on, the wind was blowing harder and harder: from occasional heavy puffs, it at last grew to be a tremendous gale. Hearing so much wind, though there were hands enough on deck to manage the ship, some of us got up to assist if we were needed. It was now blowing most fearfully; the wild howling and whistling among the rigging, the wilder roar of the angry sea, the hallooing of the captain, and the impenetrable darkness which lent its horrors to the scene, were appalling even to a sailor's breast. Just as I stepped upon deck she shipped a heavy sea, which drenched me to the skin. Presently, we heard the crash of falling timbers, and away went a top-mast, and a yard in the slings. There were now so many men on deck that we were in each other's way; some of us went below and turned in, with the full expectation that our ship would founder before morning; and thinking it would be as well to go down in our hammocks as on deck.

While this state of gloomy foreboding continued, some of my shipmates manifested great alarm about eternity. They prayed aloud, in deep distress. Others only cursed, and said, as if in bravado, "We are all going to hell together." For my own part I kept repeating the Lord's prayer, and renewing those promises so often made in the moment of apparent destruction.

At length the day dawned, revealing the sad havoc made by the winds, of our masts and rigging. We also saw a number of those dwellers on the ocean, called Mother Carey's chickens. Our shattered aspect reminded me of the *Macedonian* after the battle, excepting that we had no wounded and dead about us now. Captain Jones, who had not left the deck a moment during the night, declared that, though he had been twenty-five years at sea, he had never witnessed such a gale before. Our ship was nearly new, and an excellent sea-boat, or she would have shared the fate of many a ship in that terrible gale. As the wind abated with the approach of day, we repaired our damages and proceeded on our voyage, frequently passing vessels which had suffered as severely as ourselves. This gale was on the 9th and 10th days of August, 1815. Probably many, both sailors and landsmen, will recollect this and the September gale of that year, which occasioned such destruction of life and shipping.

Sailors are superstitious. Our men attributed this mishap to the presence of some Jonah in the ship. The man they pitched upon, as the probable offender, was an old sea-captain, who had been cast away several times. That he had done some fearful deed, was a matter of undoubted truth among them; but not being so resolute as the mariners of Tarshish, they did not cast him into the sea; neither did this liberality on their part cost us our lives, for, after several days of pleasant weather, we one morning found ourselves safely anchored at the quarantine ground, near the city of New York.

The crew of the *Siren* having obtained leave to go on shore, full of my good purposes to lead a steady life on the land, I hurried directly to Broadway, to inquire for my former employer, the kind-hearted boot-maker. To my disappointment, he had gone to Philadelphia; so that I returned on board, somewhat chagrined at the failure of my plan.

The next morning we were conveyed, in a large sail-boat, on board the *Tom Bowling,* an hermaphrodite brig. Here I was congratulated by the old quartermaster, Lewis Deal, who was with me when we narrowly escaped capture at the mouth of Salem harbor, while on a fishing excursion. He said he had felt much anxiety for my safety all the voyage, especially as it was reported that my former captain had made strict search for the *Macedonians* among all the American prisoners who were carried to England. The kind-hearted old man wept tears of gladness at my safe return.

While we staid in the *Tom Bowling,* the September gale, mentioned above, took place. We were right glad, as it broke its fury over our anchorage in vain, to think we were so safely housed in a good harbor, instead of being exposed to its wrath on the deep. Many a brave heart perished in that memorable storm.

The two years having expired for which we shipped, we were paid off. With the sum of one hundred dollars, I hurried on shore and deposited my funds in the hands of my landlord, at a sailor's boarding-house. Now followed a life of dissipation and folly. The grave resolutions, passed at sea, to settle down as steady farmers, vanished into air. Drinking, swearing, gambling, going to the theatre, and other kindred vices, took up all our time as long as our money lasted. Our religious vows were equally slighted and forgotten: instead of being better, we became worse than ever. We felt as if New York belonged to us, and that we were really the happiest, jolliest fellows in the world.

For my own part, I fell deeper into wickedness than ever before: drinking, swearing, and gambling as I had never done on any former occasion. How could it be otherwise? Who cared for the sailor then? Not one. He was left to his own depraved heart's promptings. Bethels and religious boarding-houses did not then throw their genial influences round his path, to charm his footsteps to the shrines of virtue and religion. Near the very spot where the Bethel church now stands in New York, I have frequently gambled for hours, with a bottle of spirits on the table, uncaring and uncared for by any human being. Thrice blessed be the man who first established Bethels and temperance boarding-houses! They are the sailor's life-boats, which snatch him from the gory jaws of the unprincipled land sharks who fatten on his ruin.

Sometimes, in a sober moment, I thought I would break away from this wicked mode of life. I even engaged myself to a boot-maker, to complete my knowledge of his business; but, the dread of the confinement to the shoe-bench, which my riotous fancy painted as being worse than a prison, drove me from my purpose, and left me still among my shipmates.

At last my landlord told me my money was all expended, and that I must look out for something to do. My shipmates were in a similar dilemma, their number decreasing every day, as one after another shipped in the various merchant vessels preparing for sea. Alas for our farmers in perspective. Their dreams of ploughing the land evaporated, leaving them what they were before, and what most of them remained until death, the plowmen of the ocean. My landlord's gentle hint put a stop to my excesses, for the very suffi-cient reason that it was attended with a protest on my further checks for funds. For a while, I found employment in loading and unloading ships, and in assisting to fit them for sea. But this prov-ing an uncertain employment, I was induced to join a number of my fellow-boarders in going to the rendezvous of the United States brig *Boxer*. Here we shipped for two years more. I was then eight-een years of age, and was rated as an ordinary seaman, with ten dollars per month wages. Behold me then, dear reader, once more on board a man of war, in spite of all the dangers I had escaped, and the promises I had made to risk myself no more on the ocean! The next chapter will unfold the events which transpired while I sailed in the *Boxer*.

CHAPTER ELEVEN

ON shipping in the *Boxer,* I received three months' advance, which, excepting a small sum expended for clothing, fell into the hands of my rapacious landlord. How much this gentleman contrived to filch from me, it is not in my power to say; but that he was well paid, I have no doubt. He had my hundred dollars, my advance, all I earned for working on the wharves, and nine dollars beside, which I obtained from the purser. All this, according to his account, I spent in a few weeks, with the exception of a very small sum laid out for clothing. As I had no means of proving his statements false, there was no alternative but submission, and a return to a life of toil and danger, to earn a fresh supply.

As the method by which I obtained the nine dollars, above mentioned, from the purser, will exhibit one of the modes in which seamen are sometimes cheated, I will relate it. While in the *Siren* I drew but half my allowance of grog. By the rules of the service, I could claim the balance in money. This I overlooked when we were paid off, but, when my funds got low, it came into my mind. I proposed to some of the boys, who had a similar claim, to visit the purser. They only laughed at me, and said it would be of no use, for he would not pay it now we were discharged. Finding they would not join me, I went alone to the City Hotel, where the purser boarded, and inquired for him of the bar-tender. He came down stairs, and I spread out my complaint before him. He blustered and said I had no such claim allowed; I insisted, and told him it was my right, and he must pay it. Hoping to get rid of me, he told me to call again the next day. This I did, when he paid me nine dollars. This will show the reader one of the ways in which poor Jack is plundered, and that too by gentlemen!

The *Boxer* lay at the navy yard, whither we were conducted. The vacillation of a seaman's character was illustrated before we got on board, by one of our hands running away: another went a little beyond the first. He went on board, where he pretended to lose his hat overboard. Begging permission to recover it, he seized the rope which fastened the boat to the shore, dropped over the stern into the boat, and pushing up to the wharf, leaped ashore and made off. Such fickle-mindedness is not uncommon among sailors.

We lost another of our crew in a more melancholy manner; he was in my mess, an Englishman by birth, who had just left a British vessel to enter the American service. He was at work on the main yard, and by some means or other, losing his foothold, he fell. Unfortunately, he struck a carronade screw in his descent, which inflicted a terrible wound. The poor man suffered excruciating agonies for a short time, and died. We buried him on shore, in a plain coffin, without form or ceremony. Such are the contingencies which wait to hurry seamen to the grave!

We were kept busily at work upon the brig for some time; after which our commander, Captain Porter, came on board. We soon found him to belong rather to the race of Fitzroys and Car-dens, than to that of Decaturs, Parkers or Nicholsons. He was inclined to tyranny and severe discipline.

He soon gave us a specimen of his character in a most illegal act of punishment. We lay alongside the *Hornet* or *Peacock,* I forget which. It happened that her captain and most of her officers were gone ashore one day. Our captain accidentally saw one of her men engaged in some act of misconduct: instead of entering a complaint against the man to his own officers, he ordered him to be seized up and severely flogged, notwithstanding the earnest entreaties of the offender for pardon. Why the captain of that vessel did not call Captain Porter to an account for this manifest invasion of his prerogatives, I never knew, for we put to sea shortly afterwards. An officer who would thus gratuitously volunteer his services to punish a man, must be a tyrant at heart. So at least we thought; while many misgivings, concerning the future, troubled our minds.

As I was now rated an ordinary seaman, and not a boy, as heretofore, I had a station assigned me in the fore-top, instead of being a servant to any of the officers. I was also appointed to be one of the crew of the captain's gig. This made my lot one of more fatigue and exposure than in any former voyage; a proof of which, I very soon experienced. It being now late in the fall, the weather became very cold. One afternoon, the pennant having got foul of the royal mast, an officer ordered me to go up and clear it. I had no mittens on; it took me some time to perform my task, and before I came down one of my fingers was frozen. Thus it is, however, with the poor tar; and he thinks himself happy to escape his dangers with injuries so slight as this.

The disposition of our commanding officer was still further revealed to my discomfort one day, while we were at work on the cables. Something I did, not happening to suit him, he gave me a severe blow on the head with his fist, not far from the place where I had been previously injured by the malice of the Malay boy. This unmanly blow occasioned me violent pains for several days.

Since that time, I have felt a peculiar hostility to a practice, which is lamentably common in some schools and families; I mean that of rapping children on the head with a thimble, or with the knuckles, or anything else. The practice is the result of irrational passion, it is dangerous, and cannot therefore be too severely reprobated. If it is pleaded as necessary to enforce obedience and ensure respect, I know it will fail of such effects; it will only excite feelings of revenge, ill-will and malice.

We now received sailing orders, and were very soon under weigh, bound to the Balize at the mouth of the Mississippi. On this passage we had further opportunities of learning the character of our officers. Although Captain Porter was stern and severe, yet he never used bad language. He always spoke with the utmost deliberation, but with such obvious indications of feeling, that we often trembled to hear his voice. Most of the other officers were by no means novitiates in the art of swearing; but our sailing-master exceeded all the rest in this diabolical habit. Whenever it was his watch on deck, he exercised his voice, and practiced the use of his choice and varied vocabulary of oaths, by hallooing and threatening the men continually. Whenever we had to set on sail, or to reef, he was especially diligent in these matters; mingling with his curses, threats of the lash to those who were tardy, or whose movements did not exactly suit his taste. If such officers could only apprehend the profound contempt and bitter hatred with which they are regarded by their maddened crew, they would both tremble for safety, and despise their own littleness of soul. No

really great man would enact the childish vagaries of a petty tyrant.

There was one respect in which we were more annoyed in the
Boxer than I had been in the *Macedonian*. In this latter ship, none
but the captain could order a man to be flogged; in the *Boxer,* the
lieutenant or the officer of the watch could send a man to the
gangway, and order the boatswain to lay on with a rope's-end. This
is a liberty which the laws of the navy should prohibit. A man
should be secured the rights of a citizen, as well on the *planks* as
on the *soil* of his country. True, it may be said, severity of discipline is necessary to good order in a ship. Not *severity,* but *strict-
ness,* is what is wanted. Let a strict discipline be enforced, with
pleasant looks, and a "Hurrah my lads, bear a hand!" and obedience will be more prompt and more perfect than when every order
is accompanied with a "Damn you," and with an exhibition of the
rope's-end or cat-o'-nine-tails. Common sense, as well as experience, will sustain this opinion.

While these matters were passing on board, our little brig was
dashing through the waves in fine style. We arrived at the Balize,
from whence we dropped down to Ship Island, where we took in
water. A share of this severe task fell to my lot, for I was here taken
out of the gig, and placed in the jolly-boat, to make way for a
smaller and lighter lad in the former. We obtained our water by
digging large holes in the sand, into which we placed our casks;
the salt water, by passing through so much sand, would be so
thoroughly filtrated, that by the time it reached our casks it was fit
for use. We then emptied it into ten-gallon kegs, called breakers,
which we carried on our shoulders to the boat. This of itself was
hard work, but we had certain tormentors on this island, which
made it a task of much suffering. These were hosts of hungry, gigantic mosquitoes, which assailed our persons, and especially our
naked feet, in flying squadrons, with a ferocity that indicated an
uncontrollable thirst for blood. But even these were not our worst
persecutors. They were attended by armies of large, yellow horse-
flies, which our men called gallinippers. These merciless insect
savages were always sure to attack the very spot we had rubbed
sore, after the bite of a mosquito. Their bite felt like the thrust of a
small sword; I still retain scars on my feet occasioned by these
fierce gallinippers.

This island bore marks of the battle of New Orleans; for we
found various articles bearing the broad arrow and stamped G. R.
We also remarked several mounds, which had the appearance of

being large graves. We afterwards learned that this was the place where the British brought their dead, after their unsuccessful attack on the city of New Orleans.

From Ship Island, we proceeded to New Orleans. This was a laborious passage; the current ran down the river with amazing force, bearing huge logs on its bosom, which, if suffered to strike either our bows or cables, were capable of doing much damage: to avoid them required no trifling exertions. Sometimes we endeavored to track her, or draw her along with ropes, as canal-boats are drawn by horses. But, as this brought us into shallow water, it was abandoned.

The banks of the river displayed large numbers of alligators, luxuriating on the numerous logs that were fast in the mud. We made many attempts to get near enough to these scaly monsters to pierce them with a boat-hook; but they kept too sharp a look-out for us; invariably diving into the stream before our boat got near enough for us to strike them. But, if we failed in capturing alligators, we obtained an abundance of palm-leaf, from the shore, with which we furnished ourselves with hats.

An instance of our commander's tyranny occurred while we were ascending the river. He had requested a seaman, named Daily, who was somewhat acquainted with the river, to act as pilot. By accident or negligence, he suffered the brig to strike the bottom, though without the least injury. The captain flew into a passion, ordered him to the gangway, and commanded the boatswain's mate to lay on with his rope's-end. I did not witness this flogging, for the hands were not called up to witness punishment, unless administered by the cat-o'-nine-tails, but one of my messmates said that he received at least one hundred lashes. I saw him several days afterwards, with his back looking as if it had been roasted, and he unable to stand upright. He wore the same shirt in which he was flogged for some time afterwards. It was torn to rags, and showed the state of his back beneath. His object in wearing it was to mortify and shame the captain for his brutality.

The severity of flogging with the rope's end is justly described in Mr. Dana's excellent book, called "Two Years before the Mast." Though not *so* cruel as the cat, it is nevertheless a harsh, degrading punishment. Our men used to say that "they would as lief be cut up on the bare back with the cat, as have back and shirt cut up together," as was poor Daily's. In truth, that flogging was both unjust and illegal. The articles of war provide, that not more than *twelve* lashes shall be given for a crime; but here *one hundred* were inflicted for *no crime*—for an accident, which might have happened to the best pilot who ever ascended the Mississippi. But though the captain was thus rendered amenable to the law, who would believe a poor sailor? Had he complained, it would doubtless have been to his own injury; for law, and especially naval law, is always on the side of the strong. This was not the only case of illegal flogging; but the justification of these excessive whippings, was found in the pretended existence of *several* crimes in the helpless offenders.

On one occasion we were at our quarters, exercising in the various evolutions of war; now at our guns, and then going through the forms of boarding an enemy; now running aloft, as if in the act of cutting down our enemy's rigging, and then rushing below, as if to board her, firing our pistols, stabbing with our boarding-pikes, and cutting on all sides with our cutlasses. In the midst of this excitement, the movements of one of the men not happening to please the captain, he seized a cutlass and struck him a tremendous blow with its flat side; heated with passion, he let it glance as he struck, and the edge, entering the man's back, made a deep flesh wound, which was very sore a long time. Some of our men swore that if they had been the sufferer, they would have shot the captain dead on the spot! Are men of such brutal tempers fit to command a man of war? Is it not wonderful that mutiny is so rare under such a discipline? Such an officer might do to command a crew of pirates, but not of freemen, such as Americans feel proud to entrust with the keeping of their national honor on the deep.

On reaching New Orleans, our ship was overhauled and repaired. We were sent on board the *Louisiana,* an old guard-ship, but had to cross the river every morning to assist in working on the brig. Several of our men, and myself among them, were quite sick here, owing to the free use of river water. The *Louisiana* had a number of men confined on board, for some crime; they wore chains round their legs, which were fastened to a large ball: the nature of their offense I did not ascertain.

The effects of Captain Porter's severity were seen here in the loss of two of the crew. They belonged to the gig, and ran away while he was on shore. He made a strict, but unsuccessful, search after them. To deter others from a like attempt, or because he wanted an object on which to wreak his vengeance, he gave one poor fellow a cruel flogging for what, in sober fact, was no offense at all. The man was on shore, with some others, fixing the rigging, and, for some purpose or other, had walked a short distance from the rest, without the slightest intention to run away. But the captain wanted a victim, and this served for an excuse.

Our brig being finished, we returned on board, and were soon back at our old station off Ship Island, where we found several other small naval craft. While here I saw a man flogged through the fleet, or, as this might more properly be called, the squadron. His was the only instance of the kind I saw while in the American navy, and, although his back was most brutally mangled, yet I do not think he suffered equal to those who are flogged through an English fleet. Still, the indignity and brutality are the same in *kind,* though differing in degree: a man should never be made to endure it.

Not far from our station, at a place called St. Lewis' Bay, our captain purchased some land, and actually sent some of our men to make a clearing upon it, and to erect a log house. Whether this was a legal employment of the strength and skill of his men or not, I cannot decide; but it struck me as being a perversion of the national resources to his own private benefit. Why should a captain of a ship of war be permitted to employ the time and energies of his men for private uses, while an officer of the government, who should employ its funds for his own advantage, would be charged with embezzlement and fraud? The cases are precisely alike, except that one uses the public money, the other what costs that money. It is a fraud on the country, and an imposition on the men.

A tragic event occurred at Lewis' Bay on the 4th of July, which occasioned a fearful sensation throughout the ship. I was sent thither that day in the launch. Feeling fatigued, I remained with another in the boat, which was anchored near the shore. After some time one of the crew, named Thomas Hill, came back for a pistol, for there were several in the boat, and deliberately charged it. My companion, an old *Macedonian,* named Cox, asked him what he wanted with a pistol. Hill, who was a very desperate fellow, told him to mind his own business, or he would shoot him. Cox, knowing his character, thought it best to let this insult pass, supposing he was only going off to shoot a dog or snake, as the latter creature abounded there. Having loaded his pistol, Hill went off, and we thought no more of the matter. Presently a man came running down to the boat to inform us that two of our men were quarreling. Just at that moment, we heard the report of a pistol: hurrying to the spot, described by our informant, we found a shipmate, by the name of Smith, bleeding on the ground, with a pistol-shot lodged in his breast by Hill. We gathered round him; in his agony he begged us to shoot him dead, for his suffering was not to be endured. Supposing he was dying, our testimony to his statement that Hill was his murderer, was taken on the spot. The victim was then removed to a suitable place to be taken care of; the next day he was carried on board the brig, and from thence to a sort of hospital on shore, where, after lingering a few days, he died. The murderer was seized and placed in irons on board the brig. He was afterwards removed to another ship, but what was done with him I never heard with certainty; it was reported that he was pardoned.

The cause of this fatal affray was that great instigator of crimes, Rum. The men were both under its influence; fired with its fumes, they lost all discretion, and commenced a quarrel: from words they proceeded to blows. In this struggle Smith had the advantage. Finding himself worsted, the other ran down to the boat for a pistol. With this, he returned and threatened to shoot his adversary. Smith demanded a pistol for himself, that, as he said, he might have fair play. At that instant his cowardly opponent shot him! Had they both been sober, this tragedy would never have been enacted. Who can reveal the effects of alcohol?

From this station we sailed to Tampico, where we lay but a short time, meeting with nothing worthy of remark, except that we found abundance of turtle in the river; during the day we could see their heads peeping up from the river in all directions. At night we used to send our men ashore to take them. This was done by tracking them on the sand, whither they went to deposit their eggs. We used to turn them over on to their backs, and drag them down to the boat. When alongside they were hoisted on board with a tackle; some of them weighing four or five hundred weight. They were then killed, and converted into a soup for the whole ship's company.

The day after we left Tampico on our passage to Vera Cruz, I was looking out on the cat-head or starboard bow; seeing a sail, I shouted, "Sail ho!" when three other vessels hove in sight. These were all patriot privateers, so we were ordered to our quarters; but the vessels, discovering our character, kept clear of our guns, and we pursued our own course.

About ten o'clock, A.M., we saw two more of these privateers, crowded with men, but mounting only one long gun. Mistaking us for a Spanish brig, with money on board, they fired most lustily for us to heave to. We mounted short carronades, excepting two long nines at the bows, so we bore down, all hands being at their quarters, to bring our short guns to bear upon them. Meanwhile we kept one of the long nines in full blast. I was stationed at this gun; and it being my duty to sponge and load, I had to exert every muscle and strain every nerve, as, firing only one gun, it was necessary to discharge it as often as possible. Before, however, we came near enough to injure them, they discovered what we were, fired a leeward gun in token of friendship, and hauled off. If they had not, our men very *elegantly* observed, they would have found they had taken the wrong pig by the ear.

We soon came in sight of the beautiful revolving light, which throws its friendly beams on the port of Vera Cruz, where, as in the former places, we lay a short time, and then, after visiting some other ports, we returned to our former station at Ship Island. Here, however, we remained for only a brief period, before we were under weigh for New Orleans, from which place we sailed to Havana. Such is the constant change kept up by men of war on a cruise.

On this passage, I was placed in a position which exposed me to the punishment of the lash, though by a mere accident I escaped. There was a habit indulged in among us, which is common among all sailors at sea; I mean that of stealing a nap during our watch at night. Seated on the carriage of a gun, or on a shot-locker, with folded arms, we indulged in many a minute of sweet sleep, notwithstanding it was contrary to the rules of the ship. To prevent this as much as possible, the officer of the watch used to give the first man he caught napping, a handspike, with which he was compelled to walk the deck until he found another sleeper, to whom he was allowed to transfer his burden. One night I was caught dozing, and had to perform the consequent march with the handspike. After walking about, without success, in search of a sleeper, for some time, I thought it might be well to try my fortune in the tops. Scarcely had I set foot on the top, before the officer below cried, "Fore-top, there!"

"Sir?"

"Aloft, and take in the fore-top-gallant sail!"

This order caused every man to spring to his station. Supposing no one would pass before the mast, I stood my handspike upright against it. But there happened to be a man, by the name of Knight, dozing there; and when he was aroused by the command of the officer, he passed before the mast to get on to the starboard side. As sailors usually grasp something when aloft, he missed his hold of what he intended to catch, and seized my handspike, which of course fell. To my consternation, he fell with it. Tumbling out of the fore-top, he fortunately struck the foot-rope of the fore-yard, which broke the force of his fall. When he reached the deck, he came bouncing on a tall, stout Irishman, named Tom Smith, who, not imagining the cause of so rough and sudden an assault, roared out, as they both fell together on the deck, "Och! indeed you have killed me!" Here, however, he was mistaken; he was more frightened than hurt; and the innocent cause of his fright was able to resume his duties, after two or three days' respite. Very fortunately for my back, the unlucky handspike was not suspected; and my share in this serio-comic accident remained a secret within my own breast.

It has often been a subject of surprise to my mind, that men so seldom fall from the tops, in the long night-watches they keep there. Often have I stood two hours, and, sometimes, when my shipmates have forgotten to relieve me, four long, tedious hours, on the royal yard, or the top-gallant yard, without a man to converse with. Here, overcome with fatigue and want of sleep, I have fallen into a dreamy, dozy state, from which I was roused by a lee lurch of the ship. Starting up, my hair has stood on end with amazement at the danger I had so narrowly escaped. But, notwithstanding this sudden fright, a few minutes had scarcely elapsed before I would be nodding again. How wonderful that more are not swallowed in the hungry deep!

When the weather was rough, we were indulged with permission to stand on the fore-top-sail yard, or on the top-gallant crosstrees; and, if the ship rolled heavily, we lashed ourselves to the mast, for greater safety. I can assure my readers, there is nothing desirable in this part of a sailor's duty. In whatever the pleasure of a life at sea consists, it is not in keeping a look-out from the masthead at night.

But the most disagreeable of all is, to be compelled to stand on these crazy elevations, when half dead with sea-sickness. Some suppose that sailors are never sea-sick after the first time they go to sea. This is a mistake; it is very much with them as it is with landsmen, in respect to being sick in a coach. Those who are of bilious temperaments, are always affected, more or less, when they ride in a stage or sleigh; while others are never sick on these occasions. So with seamen; some are never sea-sick, others are sick only when going out of port, while some are so in every gale of wind. Mr. Dana mentions some of the crew in his ship, who were sick, after being at sea two years, as they came to Boston. I was usually sick after laying some time in port, and have often stood at the mast-head when so sick that any landsman on shore, in a similar state, would think it hard if he could not lie abed. For a sailor, there is no allowance made for sea-sickness; he must remain at his post until it is time to be relieved.

When we entered Havana, we came to anchor near the Spanish fort, and fired a salute, which was courteously returned by the Spaniards. We had been here but a short time, before an Irishman, named Dougherty, who had formerly deserted from the Spanish garrison, took it into his head to run away from our brig. This he accomplished by the assistance of some Spaniards, to whom he made himself known. Several others also left us, in this port, among whom was our swearing sailing-master; and a great deal was said about running away throughout the ship. The man who was flogged on suspicion at New Orleans, now endeavored to get off in reality. He strayed from the boat, but the officer, meeting him, endeavored to force him back. He resisted; a struggle ensued; the officer fell to the ground, and the man called to the Spaniards to assist him. They left him, however, to fight his own battles; and the officer, having succeeded in getting the advantage, presented a pistol to his breast, and he surrendered. For this offense, he was flogged most fearfully. In the British service, he would have been hung! It is certain death with them, to strike an officer-Hearing so much said about running away, and feeling almost as unhappy as when in the *Macedonian,* I began to think of it myself. Sometimes I thought of trying to get into the Spanish garrison as a soldier; at others, of joining some of the numerous slavers that lay there, and in which our men said a good chance could be had. Sad chances, as they now appear, especially the latter; but I was young and ignorant. My feelings and the advice and opinion of my shipmates influenced me more than the dictates of an enlightened understanding. Resolving to make a trial, if opportunity offered, I one day put on an extra shirt and drew on a second pair of pantaloons. When thus prepared, the officer of the deck happened to discover the two waistbands of my trousers; he questioned me with a suspicious curiosity. I told him as specious a tale as I could invent on the spot; which was, that I had been mending my trousers, and, before they were finished, was called to go ashore in the boat, and not having time to put them away, had slipped them on. Fortunately, a needle and some thread which I had about me, confirmed my story and saved me from difficulty. It was pretty obvious, however, that the officer, though silenced, was not *satisfied;* for I was so closely watched, after that day, I gave up the idea of escape as utterly futile and hopeless.

From Havana we returned to the mouth of the Mississippi, where we captured the *Comet,* a patriot schooner, on suspicion that the patriotism of her crew had degenerated into something less respectable. Harsh as it must have sounded in the ears of her officers, we charged them with piracy; took possession of the vessel, and brought her hands, as prisoners, on board our brig. Her master's name was Mitchell; his crew were all stout, fierce-looking blacks, having all sorts of odd names, such as Monday, Friday, etc. She had a rich cargo, and contained large sums of money. It was reported that they had attacked an island somewhere in the Gulf of Mexico, and murdered its governor. We put them in irons, with sentries over them, who were charged to cut off their heads if they dared to lift them above the hatchway. I performed this duty a part of the time, parading round the hatch with a drawn cutlass; but they showed no symptoms of resistance, and were sent in their vessel to New Orleans. Their fate I never ascertained.

This adventure cost one of our own crew, an Irishman, by the name of Tom Smith, a severe flogging. Smith was quite a moral philosopher in his way; though it is to be regretted that his philosophy was a little infected with lunacy. Its premises were certainly sound, but, unfortunately, its conclusions bore but little relation to the parent of whom they boasted. He taught that man was born to do good; that his chief good was the promotion of his own interests; and that, per consequence, he should help himself to whatever he could lay his hands on, without regard to the rights of others. With these views, Tom earnestly defended the rightfulness of piracy, and could he have managed to get on board a pirate vessel, or even have contrived to wrest our own ship from the hands of her officers, and hoist the black flag, he would have cheerfully done so. But somehow, although he had made a number of disciples among his shipmates, our captain paid no manner of respect to his theories; for, when Tom, in consistency with his often declared principles, deliberately carried off a large sum of money from our capture, to his own quarters, the captain, who perceived the theft himself, ordered him to the gangway, and administered as many hard lashes, as if Tom had had no philosophy at all.

But, although Tom Smith's philosophy did not save its unlucky advocate from the unphilosophic punishment of the whip, it nevertheless exerted a baneful influence on the morals of our crew. Many of them were doubtless bad enough when they came on board; but a more complete school for the practice of iniquity never existed, than that on board our brig. Profanity, blasphemy, lying, licentious conversation, and even a system of petty stealing, were practiced on a large scale. Many of the men were ripe for any crime within the power of depraved humanity to commit, and I have often thought that even the decks of a privateer or a pirate, could not lead one faster and deeper into the extremes of wickedness, than did the influence of our main deck.

With what a voice do such pictures of sailor immorality, call for exertion on the part of an enlightened Christian community, in behalf of seamen? Where is the presence of the meek spirit of Christianity more needed, than on the decks of our merchant and naval vessels? Where would missionaries and Bibles accomplish more than here? There is no sphere of Christian usefulness so important, so promising as this. Every vessel in the navy should have its chaplain. Not one of your proud, fun-loving, graceless winebibbers, but a humble, devoted man, who Would not think it beneath his dignity to mingle with the common sailors, as a pastor among the flock of his affections, moulding their rough, but susceptible natures into the image of virtue, by the force of his pious example, and the influence of his effectual prayers. Then, in the merchant service, a species of itinerant missionary might be indefinitely useful. He might be sent out by a society, pledged for his support; and, by permission of the owners, sail in a ship on her outward passage. Arrived at her port, he might sail to another place, in a different ship, and then return home in a third. In this way, a score of devoted men of the right stamp, could exert an unparalleled influence on the character of sailors. Vice, irreligion, profanity, and insubordination, would presently flee away before the beautiful purity of religion, and our ships, instead of being designated as floating hells, would become houses of God, arks of holiness, consecrated Bethels! Pray, Christian, that this desirable consummation may be speedily attained; and be not satisfied with merely praying; add *action* to your prayers. Stir up your church to the claims of seamen! Give your money to assist in supporting sailors' missionaries, Bethels, and the like. Make it the settled purpose of your heart, not to rest until you behold the sailor elevated to his proper position, which is that of a Christian man!

CHAPTER TWELVE

AFTER a short stay at the Balize, we put to sea once more, for the purpose, as it was understood, of touching at Havana, and then returning to New York. This was a cheerful voyage; the idea of a speedy return to America, spread a feeling of exquisite delight over the whole crew, and converted the performance of our duty into a pleasure. One effect was, to set those hands, who were gifted with the talent, so highly prized in a man of war, of "spinning yarns," busily at work during every spare moment, when a group could be gathered to listen. Foremost among these intellectual time-killers was Richard Dickinson, a messmate of mine, a good-natured Englishman. He called himself the son of Old Dick, by which epithet he was usually called. Dick's powers were now in great demand, and he exercised them to our universal satisfaction, but with how great regard for truth I cannot determine. It is probable, however, that truth entered very little into Dick's productions. He was a sort of off-hand novelist; all he cared for was *effect,* and where truth failed him, fiction generously loaned her services. So bewitching were Dick's stories, that I used to long for the hour when we could lay in our hammocks and listen. My first salutation, when we lay for the last time in the port of Havana, was, "Come, Dick, tell us a yarn."

"What is the use? you will go to sleep," he used to reply.

"No I won't, Dick; I can listen to your yarns all night," was my usual answer.

Dick would then begin some yarn, which, if not so interesting as the thousand-and-one stories in the Arabian Nights' entertainments, was at least as true to nature, and, in respect to its humor, might be compared to some of the sayings of that illustrious personage, Sancho Panza, the renowned squire of the immortal Don Quixote; but, in spite of my promises, I usually gave notice of my condition after a short time, by performing a concord of nasal sounds, vulgarly called snoring, which would set Dick to swearing, and often put an end to his performances for the night.

I need scarcely say, that these "yarns" were by no means favorable in their moral effects on the listener. They generally consisted in fictitious adventures on the sea and on the shore, plentifully interlarded in their recital with profane oaths and licentious allusions. When seamen become elevated, and are properly instructed, these filthy stories will be superseded by reading good and useful literature, with an abundance of which every ship should be supplied by the benevolence of the Christian public.

On the passage to Havana, Dick and myself fell under the displeasure of the captain. We were stationed one night in the foretop, where we were comfortably dozing away the time. The captain was on deck. The officer of the watch hailed the fore-top. We did not hear him until the call was repeated two or three times. For this we were ordered below, and told by the captain that we should be flogged the next day before the whole crew. With this consolatory information we returned to our station, without the least inclination to sleep again for that watch. With a sort of philosophic desperation, I laughed and said, "Dick, which would you rather do—have your grog stopped awhile, or take a flogging?"

Dick was very fond of his grog; so he replied, "Oh, I had rather they would stop my wind than my grog, and would sooner be flogged by considerable than lose that." I question, however, if he had been left to choose between grog and whip at the gangway, whether he would not have altered his tone in favor of his grog. Still, his answer shows, how strongly sailors are attached to their beloved rum. I am happy to know that this regard is dying away, and that temperance is doing something among sailors. May it go on, until cold water is as popular in a man of war, as grog was twenty years since. We never heard, however, of our offense again. Dick was quite a favorite with the officers, and, except a blow in the head, given me by the captain, I had never been punished. Perhaps these were the reasons why we escaped the gangway.

At Havana we got a large amount of Spanish dollars aboard for some merchants in New York. These were smuggled from the shore. Our men were sent off in the boats, with their pockets and bosoms well stuffed with the precious metal; and in this way we soon got it all safely lodged in our hold, except that the captain's servant, falling desperately in love with them, furnished himself with all he could carry, and ran away from the ship.

After adding to our freight of dollars a fine supply of oranges, lemons, pine-apples, etc, we cheerfully weighed anchor and set sail for New York. We reached that port after a short and prosperous voyage; meeting with no incident, except that the cold weather caused us a little suffering, and enabled the purser to add a few dollars to the profits of the voyage, by supplying us with a lot of red flannel shirts.

When I was on board the *Siren,* I was contented. The officers were kind, the crew were peaceful and well-behaved; but in the *Boxer,* some of the officers were severe, and the crew corrupt, and I did not enjoy myself at all. Some said that in time of war the men were better treated than in time of peace; but though this may be true to a limited extent, yet I think the difference in these two brigs was owing more to the character of their respective officers than anything else. Be this as it may, my experience in the *Boxer* had completely sickened me of man of war life, and I determined, if possible, to get free of it at once and forever.

My station, as one of the crew of the jolly-boat, gave me frequent opportunities to accomplish my purpose. So, one day, at the solicitation of a shipmate, I resolved to make the attempt. Cruel treatment was my excuse; yet I have sometimes been ashamed of my course in this instance; and would heartily advise all boys in the naval service to stay their time out. We were successful in escaping; and as we had but little money, I therefore proceeded directly from the shore to a pawn shop, and there disposed of our pea-jackets, which were new, and for which the purser had charged us ten dollars apiece. We obtained the pitiful sum of six dollars for the two. With this, we started in a hack, which was to carry us outside of the city. We then travelled hard all day, resting at night in a barn, where we suffered extremely from the cold. The next day we pursued our way towards New Haven. The day after, we were still on the road. This was the Sabbath, and we felt strangely at seeing the good people of the village, through which we passed, going to meeting. The foot-stoves, that the grave matrons bore in their hands, were things I had never seen before; so, to the great merriment of my companion, I observed that they were excellent contrivances to carry their books in to meeting! We reached New Haven on Monday evening, where we put up at a sailors' boarding-house for the night. Here my shipmate left me, and I proceeded alone to Hartford, begging my support by the way, for my money was by this time all exhausted.

At Hartford I tried to ship on board some merchant vessel. Not succeeding, I strove to find some one to take me as an apprentice to instruct me in the art of boot-making, but with no better success. These repulses discouraged me. It was Christmas day, and the associations connected with the day—the merry-makings of my early boyhood—were anything but pleasant to me in my distress. The bell was tolling for the funeral of priest Strong, and it seemed as if the melancholy of the mourners fully accorded with my feelings, and was preferable in my mind to the spirit of rejoicing that prevailed among those who were keeping merry Christmas in merry mood. Perhaps, if they had invited me to partake of their cheer, I should have changed my opinion. As it was, with only five cents in my pocket, I wandered lonely and sad through the city. With a feeling of despair I stepped into a cellar for something to drink. They charged me five cents, and left me at once friendless and penniless. At the bridge, the toll-keeper demanded a cent. 1 looked at him fiercely, and told him I had nothing. He let me pass over toll free. Towards night, feeling tired and hungry, I endeavored to hire myself. But who would employ an utter stranger? I went to a number of houses, imploring a lodging for the night. With freezing coldness, I experienced repulse after repulse, until my heart chilled with horror, with the fear of spending that long, cold night out of doors. At last I called on a kind-hearted Presbyterian, who gave me a supper, lodging and breakfast. Their morning and evening devotions were peculiarly interesting to me; for, excepting while a prisoner at the Cape of Good Hope, I had never listened to an extemporaneous prayer.

The next morning I left this truly hospitable family, and pursued my inquiries for employment. Some asked if I could chop wood; others, if I knew anything about farming; and when I answered "No," they shook their heads, and I trudged on. Sometimes I offered to work for my board, but, being a sailor, and having no recommendations, people were afraid to take me into their families. Still I pushed on. A man overtook me in the town of Coventry, and began a very interesting and faithful discourse about religion. I listened respectively; he took me home with him, where, although he was a deacon, he gave me some cider-brandy: but these were not the days of temperance. After this he sent me to Pomeroy's tavern, where he thought they would hire me. This application failing, he advised me to apply at the glass works which were a little distance from that place. With this advice, I took leave of Deacon Cook, and proceeded towards the glass-houses.

Before reaching them, however, night came. A family, who occupied a red house, received me, whose hospitality I returned by singing a number of sea songs. Early the next morning, I tried to get work at the glass-house, but though I was willing to stay for my board, they would not take me. Mr. Turner, the agent, very kindly gave me a breakfast, and then I left him, determined to get to Boston if possible, and go to sea once more.

My situation was really a trying one: my only clothing was a blue jacket and trousers; shoes more than half worn out, and a little tarpaulin hat stuck on the back of my head, in genuine sailor fashion.[1] Mittens and money were alike far off from my fingers, and friends were as scarce as money. People, too, seemed afraid of a sailor; and this, in addition to all my other troubles, rendered me an object of suspicion. At such times, I assure my young reader, that the picture of a kind mother and a good home, are but too faithfully presented to the mind, filling it with a thousand vain and useless regrets. No young man need desire to be in the outcast prodigal condition in which I stood, in the depth of that cold winter.

When I reached the town of Mansfield, I called at the house of a Mr. Nathaniel Dunham; the kind manners and friendly language of whose lady I shall never forget. She told me that if I was honest, Providence would shortly open some way by which I could live. Her words fell on my ear like a prophecy, and I left the house, confident of some favorable turn in my affairs before long. At Mansfield Four Corners, I inquired of Dr. Waldo, who, with several others, sat under a piazza, and afterwards of a Mr. Edmund Freeman, for employ. They gave me no encouragement. Persevering, I at last met with a Mr. Peter Cross, who, seeing my sailor garb, asked what ships I had sailed in. Hearing me mention the *Macedonian,* he said, "There is a man here whose name is William Hutchinson. He was taken in her. Do you know him?"

---

[1] If the reader wishes to know why seamen wear their hats on the back of their heads, let him put his hat on as usual and ascend a ladder. He will find himself unable to look up until he places it on the *back of his head* as a sailor does. Sailors wear their hats thus, because they could not otherwise ascend the rigging of a ship.

"Yes," said I, after a moment's recollection; "he was our armorer's mate."

Of course, I lost no time in seeking for my old shipmate. After crossing various lots, and getting vexed and perplexed for want of proper direction, I reached his comfortable homestead. He did not recognize me at first, on account of the great alteration a few years had made in my size and appearance; but, when he did recall me to his recollection, with the generous frankness of a sailor, he offered me all the hospitality and assistance in his power. A good supper was speedily spread; and then, seated before his ample fireplace, sparkling and crackling with a cheerful blaze, we recounted our adventures. He had wandered into Connecticut, and married a very respectable woman. They now owned a house and some land, and were in tolerably comfortable and thriving circumstances. With such discourse, we talked away the better part of the night, when the old tar showed me my chamber, archly observing that "my bed would not rock much."

The next morning, he said I should not leave him until I was provided for in some way or other. Through his influence, a Mr. James, his brother-in-law, employed me to work in his cloth-dressing establishment. As I was ignorant of the business, and was not really needed, my board was to be my only compensation.

My new situation soon grew delightful to me, and I felt happier than I had ever done since I left Bladen. My time passed very pleasantly, especially my evenings, when the neighbors came in to hear me spin sea yarns and forecastle songs. Some of the young men of the "baser sort" judged me to be a fit instrument to act Samson for their enjoyment, in the house of God. So they invited me to attend the meetings of the Methodist Episcopal church in that place. But they greatly misjudged the character of seamen; who, as before remarked, usually pay respect to the ordinances and ministers of religion. I attended the meeting, but not to make sport. The result of this ill-designed invitation on myself will appear hereafter.

The winter months fled, and the spring found me unfurnished with means co-extensive with my wants. Determined to remain ashore, if possible, I hired myself to a farmer for my board. In the evenings I braided straw hats, and thus obtained a scanty supply of clothing. A little incident, illustrative of the thoughtless playfulness of sailor character, may not be displeasing to my young readers.

Whoever has seen a perfect novice undertake to guide an ox-team, may form some idea of the ludicrous adventures through which I passed during my agricultural novitiate with these horned animals. Perseverance, however, gave me some little control over our team, when, as fate would have it, my employer "swapped" them for another pair. When they came home, after some little hallooing and whipping, I succeeded in "yoking" them; then seizing the goad-stick, with as much dignity as ever Neptune wielded his trident, I mounted the tongue, (which I called the bowsprit,) and with the ladders rigged up at both ends I gave the word of command to my team. They, however, showed signs of mutiny, and, taking to their heels, bore me off in triumph. This was sport indeed; there I stood, my head and shoulders passed between the front rigging, laughing as if my sides would burst, while rakes, forks and boards were playing leap-frog, at the tail of my cart, and my master's boy was half frightened out of his wits. At length the angry voice of my master roused me from my sportive mood; he did not relish the rough usage his farming tools were receiving, and coming up with my horned steeds, he speedily stopped their speed and my sport. I need only add that his rebukes made me more careful afterwards.

When the haying season commenced, I left my first employer, and obtained the sum of eight dollars per month, and board; the wages, however, in accordance with the true Yankee method of making money out of everything, were to be payable at the village store. This change led me into a situation which proved another link in the chain, which ended in my conversion to God. The son of my employer died; he was about fourteen years of age; in company with a pious member of the Methodist church, I sat up one night with the corpse. With the faithfulness of a true Christian, he improved the occasion by seriously conversing with me on the great concerns of immortality. His discourse, together with the funeral services, had a very softening and gracious influence on my feelings, though the only present, practical effect was a more punctual attendance on the services of the sanctuary.

Towards winter, I went to live with Mr. Joseph Conant, to learn the business of filing augers and steelyards. Here my acquaintance was considerably enlarged, as several young men were attached to the establishment. Among them was one who made a profession of religion. As is usual among the young, we were devoted triflers; and he, to my astonishment, was as jocose and merry as the rest. Ignorant as I was of religion, his conduct appeared strangely inconsistent; I wondered he did not converse with me about my soul. One day I took him aside and faithfully expressed *my* views of his conduct. He acknowledged his guilt. Afterwards we attended meetings in company, and he was faithful in speaking with me about the things that belonged to my salvation. He urged upon me the importance of giving myself up to God at once, and affectionately invited me to attend class-meeting. My mind was seriously inclined, but I could not yet venture upon so close an intercourse with the people of God.

One Sabbath evening, my friend, Ela Dunham, who had dealt so faithfully with me, when we watched together over the corpse of Orson Kidder, asked me, "When do you intend to set out and seek religion?"

I replied, somewhat evasively, "Any time."

"Well," said he, "are you willing we should pray for you, and will you go forward for prayers tonight?"

To this I replied, that I would think of it. The meeting proved to be intensely interesting. My desire to express the inward workings of my mind, grew strong. Of the forms and practices of Christians in revivals, I was altogether ignorant, having never witnessed a conversion in my life; still, it seemed to me highly proper to declare my feelings in the presence of Christians, that they might give such instructions as were necessary to lead me into the right way. With these views, I determined to rise and speak, though the evil one whispered, "Not yet! not yet!" in my ears. Just as I stood up, some one, not seeing me, began to sing; this, I took to be a suitable excuse for further delay, and sat down, heartily wishing that no one had seen me. Fortunately, my friend Dunham had witnessed my movement. He requested them to stop singing, because a young man wished to speak. Thus encouraged, I told them I was then nineteen years of age, and it seemed to me too much of life to spend in sin; that eternity was a solemn idea, and I desired them to tell me how to prepare to enter upon it with joy. They proposed to pray with me. We then all kneeled down together. Most fervently did they pray for the divine blessing to rest on the stranger youth, bowed in penitence before them, and most sincerely did I join my prayers with theirs before the throne of God. After prayer, they sung the following familiar lines, which I insert both for their intrinsic excellence, and for the pleasantness of the associations connected with them in my own mind.

> Alas, and did my Saviour bleed!
> And did my Sovereign die!
> Would he devote that sacred head,
> For such a worm as I ?

O the Lamb! The loving Lamb!
The Lamb on Calvary,
The Lamb that was slain,
Yet lives again,
To bleed and die for me.

Although these words were very sweetly applied to my mind, I did not feel any evidence of the favor of God that night. The next day, with a strong purpose to live for eternity, I entered on my daily tasks. Religion was the theme of my thoughts and discourse; during the day, a sweet calm came over me; peace and joy filled my soul. It was the pardoning love of God applied to my guilty spirit.

Ah, thought I, this must be religion; but desiring to be right, I went to my employer and communicated my feelings to him. His reply rather damped my joy. He was a moralist; morality, he said, was all-sufficient to secure a man's well being both in this life and in that to come. This, however, did not satisfy my mind. To me it seemed certain that genuine repentance, and a change of heart, were all-essential to my happiness; and these, if not already mine, I determined to possess.

The remarks and experience of the Methodists, at their prayer meetings, were greatly blessed to my comfort. Gradually the light broke; the day-star shone. Peace, like a river, filled my breast; joy, as from an unfailing fountain, bubbled up within me; love animated my affections; by day and by night I sang the praises of

God, and the society of Christ's dear people seemed precious indeed to my soul. I thought this sweet frame would last forever. I determined it should, so far as my efforts were necessary for its continuance. Alas, I knew not my own heart: a dreary wilderness state was before me, and I, like many an unwary soul before me, heedlessly stumbled into its gloomy shadows.

By a sudden change in the condition of my employer, I was led to seek employment in Ashford. Here, in the shop of Mr. Giles Stebbins, I was surrounded by many light-minded, trifling young men. Falling into the same snare for which I had reproved a professor before I was converted, my peace and calm were lost, every evidence darkened, and the wretchedness of a backslider in heart filled my soul. This apostasy lasted several months, when, through the love and long-suffering of a gracious God, I was once more restored to a state of salvation. Since that time, though I have not gained all that is desirable, and that is offered in an abundant gospel, yet I have been trying to stem the torrent of iniquity, which runs through the earth, and striving to make my way to the port of Glory.

The next fall I walked eighteen miles to a camp-meeting in Thompson, Conn., the first I had ever attended. Though the scene was novel, I soon took a deep interest in the services; especially when informed that a sailor was going to preach one evening. This sailor was no other than the well-known Rev. E. T. Taylor.[1] His text was in Philippians iv. 19: "But my God shall supply all your needs;" which he handled in his usual happy and eccentric, powerful manner. I had never before seen a religious sailor; to hear one preach, therefore, in such forcible and effective style, was to me a source of unutterable delight. Nor were the listening masses before the stand, who hung with intense eagerness on his lips, less pleased than myself. They broke out into loud expressions of praise to God for his wonderful mercies. "This," said the speaker, "is but a drop from a bucket! What will it be when we drink from the mighty ocean itself?"

At this meeting I saw sinners yielding to Christ with tears of sacred penitence, for the first time in my life. Never in all my life had a spectacle more sublimely beautiful met my eye. I do not believe the world affords a more grateful sight than that of a sinner weeping and repenting before his Creator.

The parting scene of that meeting left an indelible impression on my memory. Even now I see that affectionate company marching in regular and joyful procession before the stand, each shaking hands, as he passed, with the preachers. Still I feel the tears chasing each other down my cheeks, as I grasped the hand of the sailor preacher so firmly, that it seemed I should never let it go; while he, seeing my emotion, observed, "Never mind, brother; we are on board of Zion's ship now." I had stood tearless alike amidst the waitings of the tempest and the roar of the battle, but here, among a few Christians at a camp-meeting, my heart was soft as a woman's, and my tears flowed like rain. Does the reader inquire what made the difference? I answer, it was the love of God.

When I returned home, one of my first acts was to unite myself

---

[1] Edward T. Taylor (1793-1871). From 1800 to 1817 he was a sailor. In 1819 he became a Methodist clergyman. In 1827 he served as chaplain on the *Macedonian,* which took supplies to the famishing Irish people. He was a pastor in Boston during the rest of his life, was known as "Father Taylor," and was a most successful worker, particularly among seamen.— (Ed-)

with the Methodist Episcopal church: an act which has led to the formation of many pleasant friendships, and which has proved the source of much religious enjoyment to my soul.

My mind often reverts, with a mixture of joy and sorrow, to the fate of the three hundred men and boys who sailed with me in the *Macedonian,* when I left England for the first time. Of these, alas! how many perished in battle! The rest were scattered over the four quarters of the globe. Beside myself, I never heard of but one of them who embraced religion. This was John Wiskey, one of our quartermasters. He settled in New London, and when he met in class, for the first time, he said he blessed God he had got out of that floating hell, the *Macedonian.* He afterwards removed to Catskill, on the North River, where he maintained a good Christian reputation.

My shipmate, who received me so hospitably in Mansfield, became unfortunate, lost his property, and died, but not before I had the satisfaction of offering a prayer at his bedside.

The little fellow who escaped from the *Macedonian* with me met with a melancholy fate. This I learned one day from the following paragraph in a newspaper: "Drowned, out of a pilot boat, off Charleston Bar, Mr. James Day, one of the crew of His Britannic Majesty's late frigate *Macedonian.*" Thus have I been signally favored—a brand plucked from the fire. For this special favor I hope to render my heavenly Father the eternal tribute of a grateful heart.

CHAPTER THIRTEEN

DURING the various scenes, dangers and wanderings oi these years of my youth, I had not forgotten the home of my boyhood; and, now that I was becoming somewhat settled in my prospects, I wrote an affectionate letter to my mother. After a delay of several months, I received two letters in reply, one from my mother, and the other from my sister. That from my mother is inserted in this narrative, for the purpose of exhibiting to the young reader, who may fancy that his parents feel no very great interest in his welfare, another instance of the deep, undying love of a mother's heart.

Bladen, December 23, 1818.

My dearly beloved Child:

I cannot describe the sensations I felt when I received a letter from your dear hands. It was the greatest pleasure I have enjoyed since you left me. I have never been sorry but once since you left, and that has been ever since; but I hope the Almighty has ordered it all for the best. I have never forgotten to pray for you morning, night, and many times in the day, though I talked very little about you to any one, because I did not wish to make any one else uncomfortable. But that God, who knows the secrets of all hearts, sees how sincerely thankful I am because he has been pleased to hear my prayers that I might hear from you again; for I was fearful I never should. But now I have great hopes that the blessed Lord will protect you, and spare our lives to see each other again.

My dear child, you have not stated how you came to be separated from the crew when the ship was taken, nor how you have been employed since. You must be the best judge whether it will be safe for you to venture home. It would be a great pleasure for me to see you, but if there is danger of bad consequences, on account of your having been in the service against your country, and if any bad consequence should follow your coming home, it would make me more unhappy than I have ever been yet. If there is no danger, I should be very happy to have you come home and learn a trade; as, thank God, I have it in my power to do something for you; and nothing shall be wanting to make you comfortable, that I can do. You say it may be one or two years before you come; but pray come the first opportunity, as you will be gladly received by us all. If it is a want of money that prevents you from coming, and you cannot work your passage, perhaps you can get one by showing the captain of some ship my letter, and he may depend on being paid as soon as you arrive in England. If neither will do, send me word; and if there is any place in London where your passage money can be paid, I will pay it there for *you*. You are right in supposing yourself twenty-two years of age on the nineteenth of March (1819). Your sister Maria is twenty. She is grown a fine young woman; I am happy to say is very steady and thoughtful; though not of a very strong constitution. She is at service in London. She has written to you, and I hope you will receive her letter with this.

* * * * *

I hope, my dear child, you will not fail to come home. Send me all the particulars of your life, at the first opportunity. I am afraid you have gone through a great deal of trouble and hardship since I saw you. But the merciful Lord has been pleased to bring you through the whole, and He is able to carry you through more, if you put your trust in Him. It gave me great comfort to hear that you are so well disposed, as I am sure you are, from the spirit of your letter; it was more pleasure to me than if you had gained all the riches in the world. I wish I was as well acquainted with religion as yourself; but I will try to make a better use of my time, and should it please God to let you come home, I hope you will be the means of great good to me.

There are a number of Methodist meetings about us. The people who live in our yard are very strict ones. I never disliked the Methodists; I think they have a great gift of religion. I sent your letter to Lady Churchill, formerly Lady Francis Spencer. Both Lord and Lady Churchill were glad to hear from you, and are your well-wishers. The Duke and Duchess of Marlborough are both dead. Blenheim is much altered for the worse, since his son has become Duke. Lord Francis, that was, makes a very good master; and when the Duke died, he left Blenheim. His country house is in the forest. Your father is his carpenter in the timber yard; he has filled this situation six weeks. He comes home every Saturday; and next spring they are going to place me and the children in a lodge near him. We hope to have the happiness of seeing you there.

* * * * *

It is eight years the twelfth of last July, since you left us... Your father, brothers and sisters all join with me in hearty prayers to Almighty God, that his blessing may be upon you; and if it is his blessed will, we shall see you again; if it is not, we must be resigned to what is fitting for us, and pray that we may all meet in heaven, where all tears shall be wiped away. That God may bless you, my dear child, is the sincere prayer of

Your ever loving mother,

Susan Newman.

Notwithstanding the earnestness of my mother's spirit, breathed out so ardently for my return in this letter, I dared not risk myself on British soil. Her expression of sorrow, if bad consequences should ensue, had its weight in determining me to remain; but a conversation with the celebrated Lorenzo Dow, who had recently returned from his English tour, settled the question. He said he had seen four men hung, who, like me, had been in the service of some other country, after deserting from their own. This was quite sufficient; for, much as I longed to visit the homes of my childhood, I had no disposition to do it with a gallows suspended over my head. I therefore wrote my mother, that, not having a regular discharge from the navy, it would be best for me to continue where I was; but I begged them to seriously think of emigrating themselves; since my father-in-law, being an excellent carpenter, could do well in New England. Alas! it was not for him ever to consider of this proposition; for, when my letter arrived, they were performing the sad obsequies of death over his breathless corpse. A prevailing fever had terminated a life of fifty-seven years, after a sickness of two weeks. My mother, now a widow the second time, after twelve years of pleasant union with her last husband, thought it unfitting, at her time of life, to venture across the ocean; and therefore all my plans for collecting my relatives on American soil, were blasted in the bud.

Perhaps, after following me through the changes of my life at sea, the reader may feel a little interest in knowing how I succeeded as landsman. He has seen me escaping the breakers that met me on my first approach to the shore; and now, if his patience be not entirely exhausted, he may pursue my fortunes a little further.

He left me, when my episode about home led him away from the thread of the narrative, busily at work as a filer of steel-yards, at Mansfield, Conn. From thence, I returned to Ashford, where I continued a year or two. At last, doubting the stability of my employer, and fearing lest what he owed me might be lost, I took up the whole in the shape of a wagon and a stock of steel-yards; then, purchasing a horse, I travelled from place to place to sell them; and in this manner got into a business which I have followed more or less ever since. After acquiring, by economy and diligence, a few hundred dollars, I opened a small store in Mansfield, with the intention of leading a still more settled life; though about that time my mind was strongly exercised with a desire to devote myself to the religious benefit of seamen. My sense of unfitness for so great a work, at last prevailed; and I proceeded with my plans of worldly business.

The days of which I write were those on which the bright star of temperance had scarcely shone. Ministers, deacons, Christians, all used the deadly drinks. Was it surprising, therefore, that I, but so short a time before a rum-loving sailor, fell into the common current, and became a rum-seller? No, it was not strange! But it was a strange, a glorious display of restraining grace, that prevented me from being drawn into the snare I was thus thoughtlessly spreading for the poor drunkard.

But even in those early days of temperance, I was not without my trials of mind in respect to the unholy traffic. Once, when at Hartford, making purchases for my store, of which rum formed no inconsiderable article, I accidentally heard of a lecture on temperance, to be delivered at Dr. Hawes's[1] church. This was the first discourse on the subject I ever heard. The speaker excited a deep interest in my mind, as he told of the origin of rum, its primary costliness and rank among medicines, of the growth of distilleries, the consequent decline in its price, and the attending spread of drunkenness. So deadly a plot against the peace of the world, he said, could only have been contrived in hell.

This discourse fell like a light on some dark opaque; it illuminated my understanding, disturbed my conscience. No sleep visited my eyes that night. Duty said, "Send back your team without rum in the morning." Fear of men, public opinion, interest said, "No. Every other store-keeper sells it, and so may you." The latter argument prevailed. Conscience was rebuked; the rum went to my store.

Shortly after this struggle, I married a member of the Methodist church in Hartford. We removed to Somers, Connecticut, where I continued to sell rum, though, as before, with great caution and with much inward struggling of mind. At last I could hold out no longer, and in spite of the example of ministers, (some of whom often drank, though sparingly, at my house,) in spite of the sneers of the scornful, and of the fear of loss to my trade, I gave it up! It was for the poor, untaught sailor to set the example of sacrifice to the store-keepers of Somers. Three others imitated me in a short time. Not to me, but to the grace of God, be the glory of my decision and resolution. I can assure the modern rum-seller, whose lashed and tortured soul still cleaves to the rum barrel and the toddy stick, for the sake of the profit, that I have ever regarded that act as among the best of my life.

Finding my present residence ill adapted to a successful prosecution of business, I closed up my concerns, and removed to Wilbraham, Mass., the place of my present abode; a pleasant town, but which is rendered more so by the very superior opportunities it affords for the education of children, in its most excellent and flourishing academy.

Here my life glided pleasantly and quietly along, affording no incidents worthy of special record. Happiness presided at my domestic board, prosperity accompanied my temporal enterprises, and religion reigned as the ruling genius over the whole. My ways

[1] Rev. Joel Hawes (1789-1867), for forty-six years pastor of the First Congregational Church.

were committed unto the Lord, and he directed my steps; for which I praise him with my whole heart.

In this delightful manner several years fled away; when, my business having led me, on one occasion, to New York, I heard that my old ship, the *Macedonian,* was in port. Animated with that regard for an old ship, which always inspires a genuine seaman, I went on board. She was so altered, I scarcely recognized her. Change, with an unsparing hand, had remodeled the decks and cabins, so that I felt somewhat lost where once every timber was familiar. This was rather a disappointment; however, I stood on the spot where I had fought in the din of battle; and with many a serious reflection recalled the horrors of that dreadful scene. The sailors, on witnessing the care with which I examined every thing, and supposing me to be a landsman, eyed me rather closely. Seeing their curiosity, I said, "Shipmates, I have seen this vessel before today: probably before any of you ever did."

The old tars gathered round me, eagerly listening to my tale of the battle, and they bore patiently, and with becoming gravity, the exhortation to lead a religious life, with which I closed my address. They appeared to be very susceptible of religious feeling; as, indeed, sailors are generally. Should any doubt this fact, let them hear the Rev. Mr. Chase, in New York, or Rev. E. T. Taylor, in Boston, in whose usually crowded houses of worship, the face of the rough, weather-beaten son of the ocean may be seen bedewed with penitential tears; especially at the church of the latter gentleman—than whom none know better how to adapt discourse to a sailor's soul.

During the flight of these years a constant correspondence had been kept up between me and my mother. She had constantly urged me to revisit my native land. To remove the last obstacle, she addressed a letter to Lady Churchill, to ascertain if I might safely return. She sent her the following note, the original of which is still in my possession:

Lower Brook Street, Nov. 7, 1821.

Mrs Newman,

I consulted my brother William upon the subject on which you wished for advice, as neither Lord C. nor myself could undertake to answer your inquiry; and I am glad to hear from him the following explanation in reply: "There is nothing to prevent Mrs. Newman's son from coming home; for when the war was terminated, he was safe, even if he had entered into the enemy's service; but he will of course forfeit the pay and any prize money due to him."

I am, much yours,

F. Churchill

This note relieved me of all fear, but now it had become no small undertaking for me to go to Europe. To go alone would be very expensive; but to take my family, consisting now of a wife and three children, was much more so. Hence, I put it off year after year, still writing and begging them to visit me. When the late lamented Dr. Fisk[1] was in England, he visited my mother and brother, and related to them some of the facts in my life, which he had often heard me mention. She sent me two silver table spoons, which had belonged to my father, by the Doctor's hands. My mother wrote about this visit of that "great, good man" with evident satisfaction.

At last, I received a letter from home, which decided me to undertake the often postponed and long delayed voyage to my native land. This letter stated that there was a young man in Albany, with whose friends they were all well acquainted, and that he was about to visit his mother. I found this gentleman, whose name was William Warrington, and agreed to join him with my family in his intended voyage. This agreement made, we set about making preparations for the undertaking. If the reader desires to know the events of that visit, he must consult the ensuing chapter.

---

[1] Rev. Wilbur Fisk (1792-1839), one of the greatest Methodists America has known.

CHAPTER FOURTEEN

WEIGHED down under a pressure of despondency, arising partly from temporary illness, and partly from the greatness of the enterprise I had undertaken, and whose event was so uncertain, I left Wilbraham on Thursday morning, June 3d, 1841. A pleasant passage, by the way of Springfield and Hartford, brought us into New York early the next morning. By the following Monday, the 7th of June, we were all snugly stowed in a state-room of the second cabin[1] on board the splendid packet-ship, *George Washington,* bound for Liverpool.

Before we sailed, however, I was fleeced of seven dollars by the cook of the ship. As passengers in the *second* cabin, we had the privilege of furnishing ourselves with provisions. For the sum just

---

[1] It will be *apropos* to here quote a letter from Thoreau to his sister Sophia, describing Emerson's quarters on board the packet-ship *Washington Irving,* on which he sailed from Boston in 1847: "I went to Boston to see Mr. E. off. His stateroom was like a carpeted dark closet, about six feet square, with a large key-hole for a window. The window was about as big as a saucer, and the glass two inches thick—not to mention another skylight overhead in the deck, of the size of an oblong doughnut and about as opaque; of course it would be in vain to look up if any promenader had his foot upon it. Such will be his quarters for two or three weeks," etc. Such were *first-class* accommodations six years after Leech made his voyage, with a certainty of being at least twenty days cooped up thus, and possibly *seventy-five,* as we shall see actually occurred on his return.— [Ed].

mentioned, the cook had agreed to do all our cooking at the galley, insisting, however, on being paid in advance, because, he averred, several passengers, on former occasions, had obtained his services and failed to pay him; besides, he wanted to leave all the money he could with his wife. These arguments were, of course, unanswerable, and I paid him the sum demanded. Judge, then, of my surprise, when, a few minutes before we hauled off, the captain engaged another cook; the first having suddenly made himself among the missing. Should the reader ever have occasion to voyage, he may profit by the remembrance of this anecdote.

We then hauled off into the stream; towed by a steamboat, we soon cleared the harbor of New York. Sandy Hook speedily lay behind us; the pilot wished us a pleasant voyage, and away we dashed into the wide Atlantic, buoyed up by the confidence of the hope that a few weeks would behold us safely landed on the shores of dear old England.

The details of a voyage across the Atlantic have been so often laid before the public by travelers, that they have now lost most of that interest which they would possess were they less familiar. I shall not, therefore, detain the reader with the particulars of my passage, except to quote the experience of one day from my journal.

Saturday, June 12th. Went on deck early in the morning; found it very warm. We passed two ships on the same course with ourselves. I saw a rainbow on our starboard quarter, which reminded me of the old saying among sailors, "Rainbow in the morning, sailors take warning." It was then blowing a stiff breeze from the west. All the sails were up, studding sails out below and aloft. The wind increased during the morning, with rain. We soon had heavy thunder, with sharp lightning; the weather growing squally, we took in our studding sails. Passed another ship; wind increasing with violent rain.

One o'clock, P.M. Sailors have plenty to do to shorten sail. Furled top-gallant sails, reefed mizzen topsail, fore topsail, and main topsail. We are running before the wind like a race-horse, at the rate of twelve knots an hour.

Two o'clock, P.M. More thunder and lightning, which threatened vengeance on our poor ship. The lightning is very sharp; we have no conductor up; it plays all around us, and, as it strikes the water, it hisses like red-hot iron. Several of the sailors felt a shock in descending the rigging, especially the first and second mates. We expected it would strike us every moment, but a kind Providence protected us. The sea runs very high, and the ship flies about as if crazy. We have two men at the helm, who can scarcely keep her right; it seems that she will pitch under every moment.

Eight and one-half o'clock, P.M. Sea still rolling heavily; we have shipped several heavy seas.

Nine o'clock, P.M. Wind has shifted, and the weather is clearing off.

During the whole of this gale, many of the passengers were much alarmed, and some of them spent their time in praying and crying to the Lord. How strange that men will leave their eternal interests to an hour of danger, and forget them again the moment it passes away!

The first Sabbath of our life at sea, by permission of Captain Barrows—who, by the way, was a very gentlemanly, kind commander—I held a religious meeting on the quarter or poop-deck. My audience contained all the cabin passengers, with most of those in the steerage, the captain and his mates, together with most of the crew. I told them I was not a parson, but I would talk to them as well as I could. After singing and prayer, I spoke from Jonah i. 6; alluding, among other things, to the late storm, and exhorting them not to trust to storm religion, but to become the followers of God from genuine principle. My audience favored me with profound attention. Whether they were benefitted or not, the great day must determine. It was in this same ship that the eloquent Robert Newton returned to England. He favored her crew and passengers, every Sabbath of the voyage, with one of his excellent and powerful discourses.

The following Sabbaths, owing to the weather and adverse circumstances, I contented myself with distributing tracts and with discoursing personally with the passengers and crew.

On the 26th of June, we saw the Irish coast on our weatherbeam, and on the evening of the 27th, we came to an anchor off Liverpool, after a short passage of twenty days. Here, a steamboat came alongside, bringing several custom-house officers, who came on board, and carrying our cabin passengers ashore. The next morning we hauled into the magnificent docks of this celebrated city of commerce, where our baggage was landed under the spacious sheds that surround the wharves. From thence it was conveyed, in small carts, drawn by donkeys, to the custom-house for inspection. This tedious process over, the passengers separated, each bound to his respective home; for, having passed the ordeal of the custom-house, every man is left at full liberty to go whither he pleases. I and my family proceeded to a tavern, contrasting, as we went along, the dark, dingy aspect of Liverpool, everywhere discolored by the fumes of coal-smoke, with the light, cheerful aspect of our American cities; and giving the preference to the latter, notwithstanding my English prejudices.

The next morning we all took seats in the railroad cars for Stafford, some seventy miles distant from Liverpool. After passing through the tunnel, under the city, of more than a mile in length, we emerged into a beautiful country, adorned on all sides with antique buildings and rural scenery. These passed before us like the scenes in a panorama, and, by ten o'clock, A.M., we reached the stopping-place, a short distance from Stafford. Here we were literally in danger of being torn asunder by the eagerness of two hackmen, who, as we were the only passengers left at the *depot,* were especially zealous for our patronage. A police officer, one of whom is stationed at every *depot* on the road, speedily relieved us from their importunity. Stepping up, he asked me which man I would employ. Pointing to one of them, the other dropped my baggage, and in a few minutes, we were at the door of my brother-in-law, Mr. William Tills.

Although I had not seen my sister for thirty years, yet, no sooner did she see me, than, throwing her arms around my neck, she exclaimed, "Oh, my brother!" I need not add, that our reception was cordial, and our stay with them characterized by every trait of genuine hospitality.

The town was alive with the bustle of an election; flags and streamers were floating over every tavern-sign and public building. Men, women and children crowded the streets, flushed with the excitement of party rivalry, while the continual pealing of the bells added a vivacity and liveliness to the scene, of which an American, who has never heard the merry ding-dong of a full peal of bells, can form no adequate conception. By five o'clock that afternoon, the polls closed, and the ceremony of chairing the successful candidates took place. First came a band of music, playing lively airs; next followed the members elect, richly dressed, with ribbons on their hats, and seated on chairs wreathed with flowers and ribbons, and surrounded with banners bearing various devices. These chairs were borne on men's shoulders, who proceeded through the streets, amid immense cheering from the crowds who followed, and from the ladies and citizens, who appeared waving their handkerchiefs from the windows; the members, meanwhile, bowing, with their hats in their hands, until they reached the spot where their chaises waited to convey them to their respective homes. The sight was one of great interest to a stranger, and I advise every American who visits England, by all means, to witness an election day if possible.

We remained with my brother-in-law about a week, visiting the various places and buildings whose antiquity or public character clothed them with especial interest. The town itself contains about eleven hundred inhabitants, and is the shire town of the county of Staffordshire. Its chief business is the manufacture of shoes. Among its ancient buildings, are the remains of a baronial castle, whose moss-covered battlements insensibly conduct the meditations of the beholder back to the days of feudal grandeur and knightly chivalry. St. Mary's Church is also a venerable Gothic structure, of solid masonry, whose walls have withstood the storms and changes of about ten centuries. They were about to expend £10,000 in repairing the dilapidation's of time. I heard one discourse from the curate, and was especially delighted with the grandeur and sublimity of the music from its magnificent organ, as it pealed along the aisles of the time-worn building, with an effect never witnessed in our smaller and more modern structures in America.

Here also is the county prison, modeled, in most of its arrangements, after the state-prisons of America. It contained five hundred prisoners. A lunatic asylum and a hospital, or infirmary, for the poor, are found among the products of its benevolence: the former contained three hundred unfortunate occupants.

The poor-house is a large commodious building, constructed of brick and stone, surrounded with large airy yards and gardens. It has also yards or courts within its walls, used as play-grounds for the children. The order within was excellent; every room looked remarkably neat and clean; the children were comfortably clothed, and wore an air of satisfaction and contentment. The whole house was under the control of a governor and matron who were subject to the inspection of the board of overseers, chosen by the people. One excellent rule of the house struck me as being very useful: it provided for the admission of poor travelers to a supper and lodging; requiring them, if dirty, to undergo a thorough ablution and to change their linen. In the morning two or three hours' work was exacted as payment, and they were suffered to depart. The house had its teacher and chaplain; and altogether I thought that a great improvement had taken place in the poor-laws of the country.

Having been so long away from England, everything peculiarly

English struck me with almost as much force as it would a native American. Hence, my feelings revolted at the sight of the innumerable beggars and vagrants, who crowded the streets. Italians, with their organs, white mice, or monkeys; poor barefooted children, with their baskets of matches; and, worse than either, houseless families imploring a crust for their half-naked little ones, with many a tale of sorrow and woe, were sights which greeted my eye and pained my heart every day. A sad spectacle indeed, and one which robs the luster of the British crown of many a brilliant ray. The true glory of a people is their internal prosperity, and not the extension of their territory.

The fifth of July renewed the excitement of the day I arrived. It was the time appointed for the *county* election. Similar scenes to those before described took place, accompanied with excessive drunkenness. Every tavern, and the number seemed endless, was crowded, mostly with the laboring classes, who were spending their hard-earned pence, for foaming tankards of English ale, the favorite beverage of John Bull, and one of the greatest hindrances to the progress of the temperance cause in that country; though it is hoped that the triumphs of tee-totalism will ultimately overcome this national love for John Barleycorn, as beer is humorously called in the old song.

After spending an extremely pleasant week in Stafford, we bade adieu to my affectionate sister and her husband, and, aided by omnipotent steam, we soon reached the great manufactory of Britain—Birmingham. From thence we took stage for Woodstock, subject, however, to the incessant exactions of the host of waiters, guards and coachmen, that constantly assail the traveller in England, with a request to be "remembered" for every little service rendered. The country through which we rode was delightful; all nature wore her greenest, brightest garments; the roads were level, and as smooth as the most thorough Macadamizing could make them. Soon after seven in the evening, the stage drew up at the Marlborough Arms, the very hotel from whence I started thirty years since to go to sea.

The first object that arrested my eye, was the revered form of my mother, waiting on the sidewalk, eager to embrace her much-loved, but long-absent son. Springing to the ground, I felt myself locked in her fond embrace. That was a moment of exquisite enjoyment, both to me and to my mother. Though deeply moved, she maintained a calm dignity of manner. In a few moments, she was showing the way, with the agility of a young woman, leading a new-found grandchild in each hand, to her residence, which was close at hand. Very soon we were all seated round the well-loaded board, the happiest family party in the world.

Though it afforded me and my family great pleasure to visit scenes round Woodstock and Bladen, which had been familiar to me in my boyhood, yet, as the description would only prove tedious to the reader, it is omitted. A brief account of our visit to Oxford, so celebrated for its university and colleges, may not be uninteresting.

Oxford contains nineteen colleges and five halls. Of these, we visited only Christ Church and Lincoln colleges. Christ Church is the largest college in Oxford. We were forcibly struck with the magnificence of the octagonal tower, which is over the principal gateway. It has a dome top, and is ornamented in the Gothic style, from designs by that renowned architect, Sir Christopher Wren. It is also remarkable as containing the celebrated bell, known by the familiar name of "Great Tom," and weighing 17,000 pounds. It is 7 feet 1 inch in diameter, 6 feet 9 inches high, 6 1/8 inches in thickness. I got under this massive piece of metal, and found abundant room to move about; by standing on the clapper I could reach the top over my head. This is the largest bell in England; though Russia contains several of a much larger size. I also gratified myself by a survey of the splendid picture galleries and the spacious library, the former containing some of the finest specimens of painting in the country, and the latter a large and valuable collection of books, manuscripts, prints, coins, etc.

I made inquiries of our attendant for the room in which Charles Wesley studied while a member of this college; but, although quite communicative on other subjects, he manifested a peculiar sensitiveness on this; and I declined pressing the question. After quitting the college, happening to pass the residence of the Wesleyan minister, Mr. Rodgers, I called upon him, and related to him how the porter avoided my questions. He smiled, and said that they regarded the Wesleys as dissenters, and would therefore do them no honor. Mr. Rodgers was extremely obliging; he conducted us over his beautiful chapel, and then bore us company to Lincoln college, where he pointed out the room in which John Wesley studied when a member of this institution. He also showed us the other localities of Oxford, made sacred to me by their association with the person of Wesley's grandfather, the preaching of the Wesleys themselves, and the studies of Dr. Coke, the great missionary hero of the Methodist church.

He then led us into Broad street, to the consecrated spot where Latimer, Ridley and Cranmer sealed their faith by enduring a martyr's death. Three stones mark the spot where their ashes fell; and never did I feel a holier feeling than that which thrilled my heart, while I and my family stood on those time-worn stones: the spirits of the martyrs seemed to hover around us, breathing the same high, religious determination into our minds that filled their own bold and daring spirits. That moment amply repaid us for all the toil of our journey home.

The following Sabbath I attended the chapels of the Wesleyans at Woodstock and Bladen, and in the evening had the pleasure of saying a word to my old Bladen associates, in the prayer-meeting.

After receiving the utmost kindness, hospitality and evidences of friendship from my family and friends, I took leave of them forever. Many of the neighbors, with my mother, accompanied me to Woodstock. There I wished her adieu, and when the coach whirled away, she stood following us with her eyes, the last of the company, until a projection of the park wall hid us from each other. Who could forbear a tear in such a moment? I could not, and therefore suffered the big drops to roll down my cheeks at will. There is a luxury in such grief.

That evening beheld us rolling through Hyde Park into the city of London, where I tarried a few days with my brother, by whom I was very cordially entertained. Here also I found several cousins, in prosperous circumstances whose kindness contributed not a little to my enjoyment. Having visited St. Pauls, the Museum, Madame Tussaud's magnificent collection of wax figures, and other curious and remarkable places, I took a trip to Walthamstow, the former residence of my aunt Turner. This good lady was dead, and almost forgotten by the people; her twenty-two children were all either dead or wandering, the neighbors knew not whither. Alas for the mutations of time!

A walk of two miles farther on, brought us to Wanstead, my birth-place. Here everything seemed natural, though great changes had passed over the people since I lived there, a thoughtless child. My common school teacher and my Sunday school teacher had gone to their spiritual destiny. My aunt was yet alive. My brother asked her if she knew me. Peering through her spectacles, and summoning up the imagery of the past, she at length called to mind her former protege, and clasped me to her arms, with evident gratification. It occasions melancholy feeling to see the ravages of time on the persons and places one has not visited for years!

After a hasty visit to that noble home for the worn-out sailor at Greenwich, and a glance at the arsenal at Woolwich, I returned to London.

We next visited the City Road Chapel, built by the exertions of the great Wesley himself. The sexton told us that when that wonderful man held the collection plate, one Sabbath, it was thrice filled with gold by the enthusiastic generosity of the congregation: a striking example of his personal influence over his hearers. After examining the chapel, I walked over the parsonage adjoining, and while standing in the room where, with his dying lips, the immortal founder of Methodism exclaimed, "The best of all is, God is with us," I felt inspired with his great spirit, and mentally resolved, like him to laboriously live, that like him I might triumphantly die. From this sacred chamber I visited the tombs of Wesley, Clarke, Benson, Watson, Cooper, and other illustrious men of the departed army of faithful warriors in the cause of Christ; and, as I stood over their ashes, my heart said with Peter on the mount of transfiguration, "Master, it is good for me to be here!"

Crossing the road into Bunhill fields, I stood before the tombstones of the celebrated Dr. Isaac Watts, and the less learned but equally renowned John Bunyan. Here the wicket gate, the wanderings of the pilgrim, the land of Beulah, and the river of death passed vividly before my mind's eye, until, overcome with a rush of powerful feeling, I wept and walked away, a better man than when I entered those solemn resting-places of the glorious dead.

The time allotted for my visit having nearly expired, my mind began to look towards the country of *my* adoption, filled with a strong desire once more to tread its free soil. Strong as is the love of home, it was not strong enough to induce a preference in my mind for England. America had become the dearer of the two. Indeed, I saw so many unpleasant things amidst the grandeur and pageantry of the rich, that I often felt disgusted. Such hosts of street beggars, such troops of poverty-stricken children, such a mass of degraded laborers, such enormous taxation, made me shrink from bearing any part of so great a burden, and desire to link my future destiny with the rising fortunes of America. How the laborer of England lives, with such low wages, and such high prices for the staple commodities of life, is above my comprehension. Meat was from twelve to twenty-four cents per pound; tea from one to two dollars; coffee from twenty-five to forty cents, and other things in proportion. To this add the intemperate habits of the poor, and how they live becomes a problem I know not how to solve. Yet, with all this poverty and woe, taxation is laid upon the public with merciless severity, to furnish means to maintain the splendor and fatten the minions of royalty. First, they have to pay the annual interest of eight hundred million pounds, then come the enormous salaries of the monarch and the satellites of the throne. The queen, for her private purse, has £150,000; the queen dowager, £100,000; Prince Albert, £30,000; the Lord High Chancellor, £20,000; the Bishops, an average of £20,000 each. Besides these, follow sinecures and pensions innumerable, until the resources of the nation are preyed on by the throne, with the unsatisfied appetite of the grave—taking all, and still crying, "give, give!" I felt happy, when beholding these things, that Providence had, after many trials in early life, cast my lot in America.

On the 25th of August, we all sailed from London, in the cabin of a fine ship, commanded by Captain Eldridge, bound for Boston. The particulars of our stormy and tedious voyage would neither gratify nor amuse the reader, and they are therefore omitted. Suffice it to say, that the Atlantic passage could scarcely be more unpleasant than it was to us; but, by the care of divine Providence, after being seventy-five days at sea, exposed to every variety of wind and weather, deprived of religious advantages, and surrounded only by the ungodly, we safely landed, and found comfortable quarters at the United States Hotel, in Boston. From thence we proceeded to Worcester, and then to Wilbraham, where we were hailed with joyful congratulations by our neighbors, who had begun to mourn us as among the lost at sea. Most gratefully did we all unite with the minister, the following Sabbath, in a thank-offering to Almighty God, for his goodness in preserving us from the dangers of the stormy sea.

Thus, courteous reader, I have conducted thee through the mazes of my changeful life. Should the facts detailed in these pages lead thee to feel more interest hereafter in the elevation of the sailor, my labors will not have been in vain; and should the recital of my Christian experience induce thee to embrace the same Saviour, who has become my redemption and sacrifice, I shall joyfully hail thee, when we meet together in the port of eternity.

To my brothers of the sea, let me add one word. Yours is a life of danger, of toil, of suffering. Few men care for your souls; but Jesus regards you. He watches you in all your wanderings; he woos you to be his! Will you not be persuaded, by a fellow-sailor, to heed his voice. Oh sailor, "Turn, turn, for why wilt, ye die!" Go! rest in His bosom, who says to you, "Come unto me all ye that are weary and heavy laden, and I will give you rest."

Fireship Press Editor's Note: In 1841, shortly after his return to America, Leech received a letter with the news that his mother had died.

Samuel Leech never went to sea again. As a prosperous merchant in Wilbraham, Massachusetts, he died peacefully in 1848. He was surrounded by his American wife and three very American children.

APPENDIX A

The list of the officers of the *USS United States* and their subsequent careers is as follows:

Captain Stephen Decatur, was killed by Captain Barron in the historic duel, 1820.

Lieutenant John B. Nicholson, who appears afterwards in this narrative as commander of the *Siren,* 1815, but whose name does not thus appear on the navy records. He was captain of the *United States* in 1832, and died in 1846

This list has been compiled from various sources, but the Navy Department records show an additional midshipman, John J. McCaw, who resigned Feb. 23, 1818.

Lieutenant William H. Allen, who became Commander of the *Argus* in 1813, and was mortally wounded in the action with the *Pelican* in the British Channel, August 14, 1813, and is buried at Plymouth, England.

Lieutenant John M. Funck, mortally wounded, as before noted.

Purser John B. Timberlake. Mr. Timberlake's wife, who was known in Washington as "Peggy" O'Neil, married after his death John H. Eaton, Secretary of War, 1829-1831, and became the cause of the celebrated "ladies' quarrel," as Calhoun termed it, which terminated in the disruption of Jackson's Cabinet in 1831.

Midshipmen:

Joseph Cassin, Jr., who died a Lieutenant in 1826. Philip F. Voorhees, who died a Captain in 1862.

John P. Zantzinger, who appears on the Navy List as "dropped" in 1855, but who was purser of the *Hornet* in 1815, when she narrowly escaped capture by the British 74 *Cornwallis*. In that memorable stern-chase all the guns but one, the cables, boats and nearly everything else movable, were thrown overboard to lighten the vessel. From the Congressional records we find that in 1850—*thirty-five* years after—Congress passed an act allowing Mr. Zantzinger payment for what he had been obliged to sacrifice under these circumstances, when even the knives and forks were thrown overboard.

Richard Delphy, who was killed in the *Argus-Pelican* encounter, August 14, 1813, and is buried at Plymouth, England. Dugomier Taylor, who died at sea, as a Lieutenant, October 5, 1819- Richard S. Heath, who became Lieutenant, and was killed June 2, 1817, in a duel with Midshipman J. L. Hopkins, at New York. Edward F. Howell, who was killed in the action between the *President* and the *Endymion,* January 15, 1815.

H. Z. W. Harrington (Henry W., on navy records), resigned April 12, 1813.

William Jameson, who died a Commodore April 6, 1873, his record surpassing even that of Sloat. He was doubtless the last survivor of the famous encounter of sixty-one years before.

Archibald Hamilton, who became a Lieutenant and was killed in the action between the *President* and the *Endymion,* January 15, 1815. He was son of Paul Hamilton, then Secretary of the Navy.

Lewis Hinchman (or Henchman) no record is found.

Benjamin S. Williams, no record is found.

John N. Carr, no record is found.

John Stansbury, who was killed in Macdonough's victory on Lake Champlain, September 11, 1814. George C. Head, who died a Rear-Admiral in 1862.

Walter Wooster, drowned June 1, 1813. (The Navy Department gives his name as "Winter.")

John D. Sloat, who died a Rear-Admiral in 1867, having the wonderful record of forty-four years' active service, having entered the navy as a midshipman in 1800—served one year until discharged by the peace-establishment. He re-entered as sailing-master 1812. In 1847 he secured possession of California just in time to forestall the British designs on the Pacific Coast, and was on the active list until 1855; retired 1861, but promoted until 1866—thus being on the navy list for fifty-seven years.

Surgeon Samuel R. Trevett, Jr. (died 1822), when surgeon on the sloop-of-war *Peacock*.

Surgeon's Mate Samuel Vernon, who died February 5, 1814. Lieutenant of Marines William Anderson, who died a brevet Lieutenant-Colonel, in 1830.

Second Lieutenant of Marines James L. Edwards, who resigned in 1813.

The complement of the two vessels, as given by James, was: *Macedonian,* 262 men and 35 boys. *United States,* 477 men and one boy.

If you liked this book, you'll love

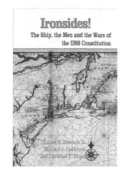

IRONSIDES!

By Charles E. Brodine, Jr., Michael J. Crawford and Christine F. Hughes

300 Pages - 6" X 9" Paperback

with 51 Illustrations

The Story of America's Finest Ship as Told by Three of Her Finest Historians

On October 21st 1797, the 44-gun frigate *Constitution* slid down the ramp at Hartt's shipyard and into the chilly waters of Boston Harbor. While the workmen were proud of their efforts, no one—but NO one—thought she would still be serving her country 210 years later.

Yet the *Constitution* remains afloat, having survived three wars, service on numerous distant stations, duty as a receiving ship, extended periods of neglect and decay, and occasional brushes with the breaker's yard. She has survived all those tribulations to become the oldest commissioned ship still afloat in the world, and a symbol of the heritage and pride our country.

Her story is told in a series of 34 short essays by three of the country's leading experts on the USS *Constitution*'s history: Charles E. Brodine, Jr., Michael J. Crawford and Christine F. Hughes of the Naval Historical Center in Washington, DC. Originally published as: *Old Ironsides: An Illustrated Guide to USS Constitution*, it is brought to a much wider audience in this Fireship Press edition

Concise • Readable • Authoritative

A wonderful resource for anyone interested in the Age of Sail

CPSIA information can be obtained
at www.ICGtesting.com
Printed in the USA
FSHW011331307721
8319F4S

www.FireshipPress.com

*For the Finest in
Nautical and Historical
Fiction and Nonfiction*